Property Hotspots in Spain

Thank you for buying one of our books. We hope you'll enjoy it, and that it will help you to realise the ideal combination of a place in the sun and a rising investment.

We always try to ensure our books are up to date, but contact details seem to change so quickly that it can be very hard to keep up with them. If you do have any problems contacting any of the organisations listed at the back of the book please get in touch, and either we or the author will do what we can to help. And if you do find correct contact details that differ from those in the book, please let us know so that we can put it right when we reprint.

Please do also give us your feedback so we can go on making books that you want to read. If there's anything you particularly liked about this book – or you have suggestions about how it could be improved in the future – email us on info@howtobooks.co.uk

The Publishers
www.howtobooks.co.uk

Property Hotspots in Spain

Where to invest in Spain for maximum return and enjoyment

Ajay Ahuja

howtobooks

I dedicate this book to Ellie. Without her help this book wouldn't exist!

Also thanks to the publishers, my Mother, Anjana, Tom and Rosa for all their ongoing support.

Published by
How To Books Ltd, 3 Newtec Place
Magdalen Road, Oxford OX4 1RE. United Kingdom.
Tel: (01865) 793806. Fax: (01865) 248780.
email: info@howtobooks.co.uk
http://www.howtobooks.co.uk

First published in 2004

British Library Cataloguing in Publication Data
A catalogue record for this book is available from the British Library

Cover design by Baseline Arts Ltd, Oxford
Produced for How To Books by Deer Park Productions
Typeset by Pantek Arts Ltd, Maidstone, Kent
Printed and bound in Great Britain by Bell & Bain Ltd, Glasgow

NOTE: The material contained in this book is set out in good faith for general guidance and no liability can be accepted for loss or expense incurred as a result of relying in particular circumstances on statements made in the book. The laws and regulations are complex and liable to change, and readers should check the current position with the relevant authorities before making personal arrangements.

Contents

A Note from the Author

Spain is certainly a hotspot! I'm sure you've seen the adverts in the local and national press offering superb properties at attractive prices. But guidance is needed. Spain is a big country! There are hotspots and not-so-hot hotspots. You need to know a little bit more than what the selling agent is telling you.

My expertise is in the UK market but the same principles hold – will you get a good rental income and will you get good capital growth? Another feature is will you have a fun holiday home? All these questions need answering. I hope this guide does this for you.

The key thing with any overseas property investment is that you get everything you want from it. The type of investor you are will determine what you want. If it's yield then go for for the high yielding all year round season properties. If it's capital growth then go for the areas that are developing. If it's a fun holiday home then go for the area with the most facilities. If it's all of these then go for the area that meets all of these – and there are areas that can do this!

If you do need further help with acquiring an overseas property then contact me on:

Website: www.spreadtherisk.co.uk, www.ajayahuja.co.uk or www.accdirect.co.uk
Email: emergencyaccountants@yahoo.co.uk
Fax: 01277 362563
Address: Accountants Direct, 99 Moreton Road, Ongar, Essex, CM5 0AR

Good luck!

Ajay Ahuja

About the Contributor

Lee Connolly was instrumental in helping to choose the hotspots for this book.

He bought his first home in Torrevieja, Spain in 1985 for only £14,500. Having spent all of his adult life working in the financial services industry he knew it was a sound investment and he now has a portfolio of properties in and around the Torrevieja area. It was through his own success and knowledge of Spain that the Spanish Property Centre was established.

Since 1981 Lee Connolly Financial Services have been successfully arranging mortgages for people in Britain and it was a natural progression for Lee to branch out into Spanish mortgages. He can offer competitive mortgages via six major Spanish banks of up to 80% loan to value in most cases for new and resale properties, stage payments and buying off-plan. He can also offer a range of commercial facilities – from acquiring premises only, to the the complete acquisition of a business i.e. hairdressers, restaurants, bars, B&Bs, etc.

Once again the company has progressed to include another sister company, European Car Hire, who provide very competitive rates for car hire. These three companies have come together under one umbrella to form the C Group.

For further information please call and quote: **CGP1** to obtain a discount on their fees on the following numbers:

Spanish Property Centre   01279 454644
Lee Connolly Financial Services   01279 626500
European Car Hire   01279 416362

What is a Hotspot?

A hotspot is an area where there are properties available for sale that fall into one of these categories:

Category	Description
A	Property prices are predicted to rise at a greater rate than the national average AND the rental yield is greater than the national average.
B	The rental yield is greater than the national average.
C	Property prices are predicted to rise at a greater rate than the national average.

I have ranked the categories with category A being the most desirable as category A enjoys the best of both worlds – capital growth and yield thus spreading the return and overall risk. Category B is ranked second as the yield is a certain outcome. However capital growth is an uncertain outcome so category C is ranked third.

I've found in my experience that investors choose category A, B or C on personal circumstances but more so on gut reaction. So trust your instincts! If you like the place then buy it. Remember this investment is not only based on financial considerations but also on whether you'll get enjoyment out of the property. To quantify this within the book is impossible. Only you know this value and you have to weigh it up against the financial considerations.

Identification of a Hotspot

So how did I identify the hotspots listed? Well the categories are based on two factors:

1. Actual rental yields.
2. Predicted property prices.

1. Actual Rental Yields

The first factor, actual rental yields, was easy. Actual rental yield is:

$$\frac{\text{ACTUAL YEARLY RENT}}{\text{ACTUAL PROPERTY PRICE}} \times 100$$

Since these figures are actuals, we collated all the rental figures from local letting agents in Spain and all the local property prices from the estate agents in Spain and calculated the yields being offered from all the locations. We then eliminated the poor yielding locations and those where we thought tenant demand was so low as not to cover the running costs of the property (even if the area was high yielding).

2. Predicted Property Prices

Here I did not predict property prices as this is an impossible thing to do. If I could do this I would not be writing this book but buying everything I could in a hotspot area! All I did was to look at what would make an area's property price rise above the national average. I came up with the following:

- Future residential developments in the area.
- Proposed inward investment from private companies, government and trusts.
- Proposed improvements to leisure facilities such as sport centres, parks and shopping centres.
- The likelihood of holiday seasons being lengthened.
- Our own experience gathered from being in this industry and from comments from letting and estate agents.

NB: All prices quoted are in Euros.

The Four Types of Investor

So, you know you want to invest in an overseas property but why and how are you going to invest in such a property? There are many ways to invest in an overseas property but I have narrowed these down into four types. Investors can be broadly categorised into one of the following and it is up to you to decide into which category or categories you fit:

Investor	Description	Profile
Retirement	This investor is looking for a home to spend either all or some of their time to enjoy the better quality of life that Spain offers.	S/he will be typically aged over 50 and be looking for somewhere that has good leisure facilities and be near the sea.
Worker	This investor is looking for a home where they can live and work so that their overall quality of life is improved.	S/he will be typically aged over 21, possibly self-employed and depending on their profession, wishing to locate to a city where there is more work, or near a coastal town where there are more leisure facilities but they can still work through phone, email, fax and internet.
Holiday	This investor is looking for a holiday home, typically used for 4–6 weeks in a year. The rest of the time the property is let out.	S/he will typically be aged over 30 with a family. Their aim is to save on holiday rental fees, rent to friends and family and ultimately pass down the property to their children.
Business	This investor is looking to buy and rent properties in Spain for profit. Their aim is purely financial.	S/he will be typically aged over 21 and either fed up with the high UK prices or looking to diversify their portfolio by buying properties outside the UK.

From reading this list you will be able to decide what type of investor you are and more importantly what you want to get from your investment. Once you are clear what you want then the whole process becomes easier as you know exactly what you are looking for.

Property Viewing Record

I have created a Property Viewing Record that can be a useful aide-mémoire to have with you when going to look at potential investments:

Property Viewing Record
Estate Agent/Auctioneer
Address of the Property
Type of Property
Asking Price
Date of first viewing
Date of second visit
Comments about the Surrounding Area
Schools   Traffic Noise   Shops   Public Transport   Business Units
Outside
Garden and Driveway
Garage
Window Frames/Glass
Walls
Drains/Guttering
Roof
Neighbouring Properties

Inside
Hallway
Lounge
Dining Room
Kitchen
Utility Room
Bedroom 1 (Sizes)
Bedroom 2
Bedroom 3
Bedroom 4
Bathroom
Loft
Potential Work Required
Heating and Plumbing
Electrical Repair
Decoration
Damp Patches
External Lighting
General Observations/Things to Remember

How to Use the Property Hotspot Profiles

Before you explore all the property hotspot profiles I've prepared for you, here is an explanation of what headings I used for each hotspot, what they mean and why I've included them.

Heading	Description	Why included
Area	The area in Spain where the hotspot is.	You need to know where the hotspot is!
Investor profile	The investor profiles to which the area is suited. See 'The Four Types of Investor' for definitions.	There's no point looking at a hotspot if it doesn't match the type of investor you are. Ensure that the hotspot is relevant to you.
Category	The quality of hotspot – see 'What is a Hotspot?' for definitions.	Some hotspots are better than others. I have graded them to help you match them with your personal goals.
Total population	The population aged over 15 in the hotspot.	Gives you an idea to the size of the area based on population of people.
Total British population	The population aged over 15 in the hotspot that are British.	Gives you an idea of how British an area is based on population of British people.
Hours of sunshine per day in summer	Average number of hours of sunshine per day for the summer months.	Gives you an indication of the quality of climate you might expect from the area.
Days of rain per year	Average number of days of rain during the year.	Gives you an indication of the quality of climate you might expect from the area.
Average Spring air temperature	Average temperature for the Spring season.	Gives you an indication of the quality of climate you might expect from the area.
Average Summer air temperature	Average temperature for the Summer season.	Gives you an indication of the quality of climate you might expect from the area.

Heading	Description	Why included
Average Autumn air temperature	Average temperature for the Autumn season.	Gives you an indication of the quality of climate you might expect from the area.
Average Winter air temperature	Average temperature for the Winter season.	Gives you an indication of the quality of climate you might expect from the area.
Average water temperature	Average temperature of the sea during the Summer season.	Gives you an indication of the quality of climate you might expect from the area.
Proximity to airport	How close the area is to an airport and which one.	You need to know where to fly to and whether it's a walk or a drive to get to the area.
Proximity to beach	How close the area is to the beach.	If you are going for the sun you need to know how far the beach is from the area.
Proximity to nearest city	How close an area is to a main city.	Sometimes the area doesn't have all the facilities that a city has. That's why its handy to know how far away the closest city is.
Number of universities	The number of higher education facilities in the area.	If you're looking to buy a property to rent out to students then knowing whether the area has a university is helpful.
Number of international schools	The number of international education facilities in the area.	If you intend to move here and send your children to an English speaking school you need to know which areas have these schools.
Number of private schools	The number of private education facilities in the area.	If you want to send your children to a fee-paying school then you need to know which areas have these schools.
Number of public hospitals	The number of public medical facilities in the area.	It's important to know whether the area has a hospital if you are concerned about possible ongoing medical treatment.
Number of private hospitals	The number of private medical facilities in the area.	If you wish to pay for your healthcare then you will need to know whether there are any private hospitals in the area.
Number of private clinics	The number of private clinics in the area.	If you wish to pay for your healthcare then you will need to know whether there are any private clinics in the area.

Heading	Description	Why included
Number of shopping centres	The number of shopping centres in the area.	This gives you an idea of how many places there are to shop and whether the area is self-sufficent.
Number of markets	The number of markets in the area.	This gives you an idea of how many places there are to shop and whether the area is self-sufficent.
Restaurants and bars	The type of restaurants in and near the area.	This gives you an indication of the range and variety of cuisines available which helps you set the scene of the major high streets.
Sports and leisure facilities	The sport and leisure facilities in and near the area.	If you go on holiday you want to have fun! It's good to know what's on offer so you can decide on an area.
Transport	The public transport and road connections in the area.	You need to know how easy it is to get about and around the area and how easy it is to get out of the area as well!
Crime rate	The crime rate for all types of crime expressed as low, medium or high.	Data is a bit limited on the crime rates. I have ranked them as low, medium and high from what I could find out. It's important to know whether there is a problem. Crime rate in Spain is high generally so don't be put off if an area has a stated high crime rate. If an area is low then consider this a bonus.
Main types of employment	The typical types of employment opportunities in the area.	If you wish to work in the area then it's good to know what type of employment opportunities are available.
Future plans	The proposed future developments in the area.	The likelihood of capital growth is dependent on the future developments in the area.
Yield range	The range of yields available in the area. Yields being the annual rent/purchase price x 100%.	This gives you an idea of the range of yields to expect from your property. From this you can gauge whether this meets your specific investment goals.
Entry price	The cheapest price you would expect to pay for that type of property in the area. Prices are in Euros.	This is a guide price to let you know how much, at a minimum, you'll need to have to get each type of property.

Heading	Description	Why included
Rent – school holiday peak	The rent per week for the 6 week period over the summer and if applicable 1 week in Easter and 3 weeks in winter when the schools break for holidays. This equates to the last week in July, the 4 weeks in August, the first week in September, the 3 weeks straddling Christmas and the Easter bank holiday weekend.	This is a guide price of typical weekly rental prices you could charge. From this you can determine your return from your holiday investment.
Rent – peak	The rent per week for the 10 week period either side of the school holiday peak. This equates to all of June, the first 3 weeks in July and the last 3 weeks in September.	This is a guide price of typical weekly rental prices you could charge. From this you can determine your return from your holiday investment.
Rent – off peak	The rent per week for all the other periods that do not fall in the two periods above.	This is a guide price of typical weekly rental prices you could charge. From this you can determine your return from your holiday investment.
Average annual yield	I have assumed full occupancy in the school holiday and peak periods but only 10 weeks' occupation for the off-peak season. This equates to a 30 week occupation for the property. So average annual yield is: (30 weeks rent for the year/entry property price) x 100%.	This gives you the average yield for each type of property. You can use these figures to decide whether the area and the type of property is right for you.
Demand for letting school holiday peak	My opinion of the demand for rental properties in the school holiday peak season.	You can gauge how risky the investment is based on the likely demand for your property.
Demand for letting peak	My opinion of the demand for rental properties in the peak season.	You can gauge how risky the investment is based on the likely demand for your property.
Demand for letting off-peak	My opinion of the demand for rental properties in the off-peak season.	You can gauge how risky the investment is based on the likely demand for your property.
Financial and leisure score out of 10	The total score of the finance and leisure scores.	A simple score out of ten for an easy determination of the quality of the hotspot based on the financial and leisure factors.

Heading	Description	Why included
Financial score out of 5	Based on yields and scope for capital growth a score out of 5 is given for potential profit.	A simple score out of five for an easy determination of the quality of the hotspot based on the financial factors.
Leisure score out of 5	Based on the facilities, restaurants and amenities a score out of 5 is given for potential fun.	A simple score out of five for an easy determination of the quality of the hotspot based on the leisure factors.
Flights scheduled from	All the airports that fly to the area.	You need to know how easy it is to get to the area from where you live in the UK.
Typical cost of flights	Typical cost of flights to the area.	You need to know whether trips to your holiday home will cost you pennies or a small fortune!
Operators	The airlines that fly to the area.	It's good to know the operators so you can contact them direct for even cheaper flights.
Description	A description of the area.	Okay, I've given you the statistics but its only fair that I give you some words about the area!
Hot website	The best website I've found that will give you more information.	Don't just take my book as your only source of information. Make your own independent enquiries starting on the web with this site.
Estate agents	A list of the estate agents that sell property in the area.	You need to know where to buy the properties from!
Letting agents	A list of the letting agents that let and manage properties in the area.	If you decide to let then you'll need some help. These companies should be able to assist.

All information given is correct at the time of going to press but readers are advised to check the current situation.

A–Z of Property Hotspots in Spain

A Coruña, Galicia

Investor profile:	Worker, Business						
Category:	A						
Population:	**Total** 240,000				**British** 4,000		
Climate:	Hours of sunshine per day in summer	Days of rain per year	Average spring air temp.	Average summer air temp.	Average autumn air temp.	Average winter air temp.	Average water temp.
	7	170	12	18	16	11	13
Proximity to:	**Airport** 40 miles (Santiago)		**Beach** 0.25 miles		**Nearest city** A Coruña		
Educational facilities:	Number of universities		Number of international schools		Number of private schools		
	0		1		20		
Health services:	Number of public hospitals		Number of private hospitals		Number of private clinics		
	2		5		10		
Shopping:	Number of shopping centres			Number of markets			
	2			5			
Restaurants and bars:	Over 360 restaurants in the area. Many bars in the main square – Plaza Maria Pita.						
Sports and leisure facilities:	2 flying clubs. 2 diving clubs. 2 golf clubs, one with additional tennis court and swimming pool. 4 horse riding clubs. 2 sailing clubs. 3 tennis clubs. Bazan museum near port. Archaeology Museum, Science Museum and Museum of Mankind. Fine Art Gallery. Finisterrae Aquarium with more than 300 species of fish.						
Transport:	**Public transport** Domestic bus services to Barcelona, Madrid and Andalucia. Local bus services to metropolitan area. Also buses to Santiago and Ferrol. Train services to Madrid, Barcelona, Santiago and Ferrol.			**Roads** A-9 motorway from Santiago de Compostela. C-642 and N-634 from Santander. E-70 and N-VI from Leon. North-west motorway to Madrid.			
Crime rate:	Low.						
Main types of employment:	Fish, livestock and wine exports. Steelworks. Tobacco-pressing.						
Future plans:	None.						
Yield range:	11.5%–12.9%						

Type of property:	Entry price	Rent – school holiday peak	Rent – peak	Rent – off peak	Average annual yield
2 bed apartment	76,492.27	405	324	194	12.1%
3 bed apartment	91,790.73	486	389	233	12.1%
3 bed townhouse	114,738.4	648	518	311	12.9%
Villa	168,283	851	680	408	11.5%

Demand for letting:	School holiday peak High		Peak High		Off peak High

Finance and leisure scores:	Financial (out of 5) 4	Leisure (out of 5) 5	Total (out of 10) 9

Flights scheduled from:	Gatwick, Heathrow, London City, Bristol, Cardiff, Newquay, Plymouth, Southampton, Birmingham, Norwich, Humberside, Newcastle, Teesside, Manchester, Aberdeen, Edinburgh, Glasgow, Inverness, Guernsey, Jersey, Leeds/Bradford, Belfast City.

Typical cost of flights:	School holiday peak £190–1,378	Peak £141–1,021	Off peak £106–766

Operators:	BA, BMI, Air Europa, Iberia

Description:	A Coruña is an important trading and administrative centre. Formerly known as La Coruña, A Coruña is an attractive, old maritime city located on the north-west coast. It has a busy harbour and an old quarter nicknamed 'the Groyne'. It has 4 long sandy beaches with cliffs and coves and a range of amenities. Inland is hilly and green. Monuments in the old town include several churches e.g. 12th-century Church of Santiago; the 13th-century Church of Santa María del Campo. The Tower of Hercules lies at the port of Coruña and is the oldest fully working lighthouse in the world.
	It is also one of the cheapest places to live in Spain. As a result you get double digit yields which only improve due to the season being all year round. Entry price for a 2 bed flat is only £50k so this part of Spain is accessible to most. This area does make good business investments. Employment is high, demand for rental properties are high and the scope for capital growth is almost definite.
	From Dover the area is driveable to (approx 11 hours) so can be easily accessed without the need to book flights for the whole family. It has some of the facilities you would find at the better southern resorts, but not all. It has some facilites that you wouldn't find in these southern resorts such as classical Spanish cinemas and traditional religious festivals.

Hot website:	http://www.aytolacoruna.es

Estate Agents:	Name	Address	Tel	Web
	Apartments Bellavista	Aritas Brens-Cee 15270, A Coruña	Tel and Fax: 0034 981 745 237	http://finisterrae.com/apartaments/bellaeng.htm email: bellavista@finisterrae.com

Estate Agents:	Name	Address	Tel	Web
	Tano	A Coruña Galicia A Coruña	0034 659 950 307	http://www. arrakis.es/ ~tano/ anuncios.html email: tano@ arrakis.es
	Rivas Inmobiliaria	C/ Real 20 15402 Ferrol A Coruña	0034 981 324 592/Fax: 0034 981 319 551	http://www. inmorivas.com email: rivas@ inmorivas.com
	Agencia Carballido	Calle Huertas, nº1, 1ºB, 15003 A Coruña	0034 981 226 759/Fax: 0034 981 211 290	Not disclosed
Letting Agents:	Name	Address	Tel	Web
	Sitia. Inmobiliaria Financiera	Calle Monforte, nº 15, 1º 15007 A Coruña	0034 981 248 087/Fax: 0034 981 248 011	http://www. sitia.com email: attcliente @sitia.com
	Urbher.S.L	Calle Caballeros, nº 25, 15009 A Coruña	0034 981 151 699/Fax: 0034 981 151 699	http://Sr. Alborés email: urbher@ cemiga.es
	EL EO	Alcalde Marchesi, nº 2, 1º, 15006 A Coruña	0034 981 133 271	Not disclosed
	Urbanizadora Herculina S.L. (Urbher)	Calle Caballeros, nº 25 Entrplta 15008 A Coruña	0034 981 151 699/Fax: 0034 981 151 699	email: urbher@ mundo-r.com

Alcudia, Majorca		
Investor profile:	Retirement, Worker, Holiday, Business	
Category:	C	
Population:	**Total** 13,800	**British** 2,500

Climate:	Hours of sunshine per day in summer	Days of rain per year	Average spring air temp.	Average summer air temp.	Average autumn air temp.	Average winter air temp.	Average water temp.
	11	65	19	24	21	15	16

Proximity to:	Airport 33.75 miles (Palma)	Beach 0.25 miles	Nearest city 33 miles (Palma)
Educational facilities:	Number of universities 0	Number of international schools 0	Number of private schools 0
Health services:	Number of public hospitals 0	Number of private hospitals 1	Number of private clinics 2

Shopping:	Number of shopping centres 0	Number of markets 2

Restaurants and bars:	Fast food and British food is predominantly available in Port d'Alcudia. However a good selection of fish restaurants can be found around the harbour.	
Sports and leisure facilities:	Watersports. Tennis courts. Squash clubs. Hidropark water-park. National park of S'Abufera inland from Port d'Alcudia.	

Transport:	**Public transport** Regular bus services along the beach and to Puerto de Pollensa and Ca'n Picafort.	**Roads** C-713 from Palma. Also main road links from Arta and Manacor.

Crime rate:	High
Main types of employment:	Service sector.
Future plans:	Restricted.
Yield range:	6.1%–6.8%

Type of property:	Entry price	Rent – school holiday peak	Rent – peak	Rent – off peak	Average annual yield
2 bed apartment	218,550	610	488	293	6.4%
3 bed apartment	262,260	732	586	351	6.4%
3 bed townhouse	327,825	976	781	468	6.8%
Villa	480,810	1,281	1,025	615	6.1%

Demand for letting:	School holiday peak High	Peak Medium	Off peak Low

Finance and leisure scores:	Financial (out of 5) 2	Leisure (out of 5) 3	Total (out of 10) 5

Flights scheduled from:	Gatwick, Luton, Stansted, Norwich, Southampton, Bournemouth, Exeter, Bristol, Cardiff, Birmingham, East Midlands, Manchester, Liverpool, Leeds/Bradford, Humberside, Teesside, Newcastle, Glasgow, Edinburgh and Aberdeen.

Typical cost of flights:	School holiday peak £115–470	Peak £85–348	Off peak £64–261

Operators:	Air Europa, BMI, Iberia, BA, Air-Berlin, Easyjet, My Travel, Futura, Thomas Cook, Excel Airways, Britannia Airways, Monarch, Air Europa, Air2000, Flyjet.

Description:	Alcudia is a resort located on the north east coast, situated in a bay called Port d'Alcudia. The coastline within the bay is built up with many hotels and apartment blocks, forming a resort popular with the British. There are 7 miles of beaches in the resort – the longest stretch on the island. Alcudia also has an historic, walled old town with Roman remains. Like the rest of Majorca, property in the area is relatively expensive but you do get a good rent for the peak periods. Majorca is here to stay so acquiring a property here, in the long term, is of relatively low risk. You can easily get flights to this area so it will always appeal to the package holidaymaker. The season is longer than most but not all year round. There are many villas for sale and a lot can be had for your money. The re-sale market is quite developed and there are bargains popping up every now and again. I would suggest buying at least half a mile inland or more from the coast as you get better value for money compared to the sea front properties.

Hot website:	http://www.mallorcaweb.com/eng/index.html

Estate Agents:	Name	Address	Tel	Web
	The Prestige Property Group	No Address	01935 817 188 Fax: 01935 817 199	http://www.prestige property.co.uk email: sales@ prestige property.co.uk

Estate Agents:	Name	Address	Tel	Web
	Escape 2 Balearics	Hamilton House, 205 Bury New Road, Whitefield, M45 7EJ	0161 280 7375 Fax: 0161 959 5680	http://www. escape2 balearics.co.uk/
	Interealty Balearics	Plaza Santa Ponsa, 4 Local 1 en E-07180, Santa Ponsa, Mallorca	0034 971 699 545/Fax: 0034 971 699 556	www.interealty-mallorca.com
	Roberto Jaime Gourlay	Apartado 1423, Palma De Mallorca	0034 971 681 873/Fax: 0034 971 680 320	http://www. mallorca-real-estate.com email: robertog @ocea.es.com/
Letting Agents:	Name	Address	Tel	Web
	Interealty Balearics	Plaza Santa Ponsa, 4 Local 1 en E-07180, Santa Ponsa, Mallorca	0034 971 699 545/Fax: 0034 971 699 556	www.interealty-mallorca.com.
	Europa Inmobiliaria	Antoni Maria Alcover nº 47 Palma	0034 971 676 787/Fax: 0034 971 676 567	http://www. europa-inmobiliaria. email: europa @europa-inmobiliaria. com
	Arko Inmobiliario	Avda. Son Rapinya, nº 8 1º C, Palma de Mallorca	0034 619 226 688/971 453 689/Fax: 0034 971 457 900	email: arco inmobiliario@ hotmail.com

Alicante, Costa Blanca

Investor profile:	Retirement, Worker, Holiday, Business						
Category:	C						
Population:	Total 278,000				British 10,000		
Climate:	Hours of sunshine per day in summer	Days of rain per year	Average spring air temp.	Average summer air temp.	Average autumn air temp.	Average winter air temp.	Average water temp.
	11	42	21	30	24	17	18
Proximity to:	Airport 7 miles (Alicante)		Beach 0.25 miles		Nearest city Alicante		
Educational facilities:	Number of universities		Number of international schools		Number of private schools		
	1		0		3		
Health services:	Number of public hospitals		Number of private hospitals		Number of private clinics		
	1		5		10		
Shopping:	Number of shopping centres			Number of markets			
	3			3			

Restaurants and bars:	Most variety is located in the old town and near the promenade (Explanada), and also around the port and the marina. As well as local Valencian food, international food also available.
Sports and leisure facilities:	3 golf courses in area. Marina with Alicante-Costa Blanca Nautical Club and Royal Nautical and Regatta Club. Theme park on Tossal mountain next to San Fernando castle with mini golf, bowls, skating and skateboarding areas. Flying lessons at private airfield in Muchamiel. Casino. Concerts at the Explanada. 10 cinemas. 2 theatres. Plays, operas and dance shows at the Teatro Principal. Live music shows in the old town (El Barrio). Alicante Bullfighting museum, MARQ archaeological museum, Gravina Fine Arts museum (MUBAG) and Pozos de Garrigós (Water museum). 3 main nightlife areas: behind the Esplanada ('la zona'), 'Ruta de la Madera' and 'El barrio'. Parks: La Ereta Park, Canelejas Park, Parque del Oueste, Parque del Morant and Palmeral.

Transport:	**Public transport** Train and bus services from Madrid, Murcia and Valencia. Bus services within the city (over 25 routes), and to rest of Costa Blanca. Trains within and around the city.	**Roads** N-332 from Benidorm and Valencia. Also A-7 from Valencia and Murcia. A-92, N-340 then A-7 from Granada.
Crime rate:	High	

Main types of employment:	Mostly professional.				
Future plans:	Alicante 2020-redevelopment plan involving improved access (including disabled access) to city. Improvement of transport systems by building train connection to airport and extending the high-speed train line from Valencia. Also expansion of green areas.				
Yield range:	6.9%–8.1%				
Type of property:	Entry price	Rent – school holiday peak	Rent – peak	Rent – off peak	Average annual yield
2 bed apartment	147,250	526	421	252	8.1%
3 bed apartment	184,063	631	505	303	7.8%
3 bed townhouse	276,094	842	673	404	6.9%
Villa	323,950	1,105	884	530	7.8%
Demand for letting:	School holiday peak High		Peak High		Off peak High
Finance and leisure scores:	Financial (out of 5) 3		Leisure (out of 5) 5		Total (out of 10) 8
Flights scheduled from:	Gatwick, Heathrow, London City, Luton, Stansted, Bristol, Cardiff, Exeter, Newquay, Plymouth, Bournemouth, Southampton, Birmingham, East Midlands, Humberside, Newcastle, Teesside, Blackpool, Isle of Man, Liverpool, Manchester, Aberdeen, Edinburgh, Glasgow, Inverness, Belfast City, Belfast International, Derry, Cork, Dublin, Guernsey, Jersey, Norwich, Leeds/Bradford.				
Typical cost of flights:	School holiday peak £192–485		Peak £142–359		Off peak £107–269
Operators:	Monarch, Iberia, BA, BMI, Air-Berlin, Thomas Cook, Easyjet, Flybe, Excel Airways, Britannia Airways, Futura, European Air Charter, My Travel, Astraeus, Air2000.				
Description:	An historical city and major port of Spain. Sights include Santa Barbara Castle, Santa María Church, San Nicholas de Bari Co-Cathedral, the Santa Faz Monastery, the remains of the Iberian settlement on Tossal de Manises and the Explanada – a tree-lined, marbled promenade.　　Several beaches on city outskirts. San Juan de Alicante beach to east of city is over 5 miles long. There are 5 more beaches in the area and all are Blue Flag (clean and high standard).　　Traffic congestion, noise and pollution however a problem, along with rising crime rate. The old quarter (known as Santa Cruz) has narrow streets which can be dangerous as well as picturesque.　　Residential areas surround the city e.g. Carolinas to the north-east, and Albufereta, Dos Bahias and Nuevo Alicante to the east. Property in the city centre is more expensive than on the outskirts so these residential areas can prove more value for money. There is an excellent transport system that supports the city so getting around will never be a problem. Road connections have improved significantly over the last 5 years and will continue to do so.				

Hot website:	http://www.alicanteturismo.com/ing/fr_home.htm			
Estate Agents:	**Name**	**Address**	**Tel**	**Web**
	Advanta Homes S.L.	Apartado de Correos 1632, Elche 03200 Alicante	0800 652 8890/0034 965 457 772 (Spain)	Not disclosed
	Amics Properties	Calle Cartegena 18 bajo, 03140 Guardamar del Segura, Alicante	0034 965 729 883/Fax: 0034 965 728 613	Not disclosed
	Bellevue	Avda. Maisonnave 46, 2 nº C, 03003 Alicante	0034 965 229 927/Fax: 0034 965 121 006	Not disclosed
	Immo Prestigi	Calle La Pinta 1, 03710 Calpe, Alicante	0034 965 839 792/Fax: 0034 965 839 793	Not disclosed
Letting Agents:	**Name**	**Address**	**Tel**	**Web**
	Sajonia	Avda. Alfonso el Sabio, 16, 8-Izq Alicante	0034 965 230 627/Fax: 0034 965 230 627	email: sajonia21 @yahoo.es
	Agencia Inmobiliaria Heral2	Avda. Dpto. Kiko Sanchez, 1 – local 7 Alicante	0034 965 163 554 Fax: 0034 965 260 751	http://www. heral2.com email: heral2@ terra.es
	ServiCasa	C/ Azorin, 4 – Bajo Alicante	0034 965 105 735/Fax: 0034 965 110 5601	http://www. interpisos. com/servicasa email: servicasa3 @hotmail.com
	EuroCasa Gestion Inmobiliaria	Aptdo. Correos 2053 Alicante	0034 655 169 971	email: daniel combret@ yahoo.es

Almeria, Costa de Almeria

Investor profile:	Retirement, Worker, Holiday, Business						
Category:	C						
Population:	**Total** 160,000					**British** 3,000	
Climate:	Hours of sunshine per day in summer	Days of rain per year	Average spring air temp.	Average summer air temp.	Average autumn air temp.	Average winter air temp.	Average water temp.
	11	7	20	30	22	16	20
Proximity to:	**Airport** 6 miles (Almeria)		**Beach** 0.25 miles			**Nearest city** Almeria	
Educational facilities:	Number of universities 0		Number of international schools 0			Number of private schools 6	
Health services:	Number of public hospitals 2		Number of private hospitals 1			Number of private clinics 7	
Shopping:	Number of shopping centres 2				Number of markets 4		
Restaurants and bars:	Many bars and expensive restaurants. International food widely available. Local speciality is fish and seafood. Many grill bars and also many wine bars serving the region's local wine.						
Sports and leisure facilities:	Deep-sea diving, sport-fishing, jet-skiing, water-skiing, sailing, windsurfing. 7 yacht clubs. 4 golf courses. Fishing port. Public and private tennis courts. 5 horse riding centres. Also parachuting, mountain-biking and rock-climbing clubs. 3 parks: Cabo de Gata park east of city with quiet beaches and coves, Sierra Nevada park with year-round snow and Sierra Maria Los-Velez park to the north of the city with castle and caves. Albufera of Adra natural reserve. La Envia golf course in Sierra de Gador behind city. 3 historical museums displaying local Roman and Iberian remains.						
Transport:	**Public transport** Trains from Granada, Barcelona, Seville, Cadiz and Madrid. Limited bus service from Granada, Malaga and Murcia.			**Roads** N-340 from Costa del Sol/Malaga. N-324 motorway from Granada.			
Crime rate:	Low						
Main types of employment:	Agriculture and tourism.						

Future plans:	New sports facilities (for the forthcoming Mediterranean Games in 2005). More golf courses. More tourist complexes.				
Yield range:	9.3%–10.9%				
Type of property:	Entry price	Rent – school holiday peak	Rent – peak	Rent – off peak	Average annual yield
2 bed apartment	120,202	575	460	276	10.9%
3 bed apartment	150,253	690	552	331	10.5%
3 bed townhouse	225,379	920	736	442	9.3%
Villa	264,444	1,208	966	580	10.4%

Demand for letting:	School holiday peak Med	Peak Med	Off peak Low
Finance and leisure scores:	Financial (out of 5) 3	Leisure (out of 5) 4	Total (out of 10) 7

Flights scheduled from:	Gatwick, Heathrow, Luton, Stansted, Bristol, Cardiff, Birmingham, East Midlands, Newcastle, Teesside, Liverpool, Manchester, Leeds/Bradford, Glasgow, Inverness, Belfast International, Dublin.

Typical cost of flights:	School holiday peak £259–828	Peak £192–613	Off peak £144–460

Operators:	Iberia, BA, BMI, European Air Charter, Thomas Cook, Monarch, Air 2000, Britannia Airways, Excel Airways, My Travel.
Description:	The city of Almeria is situated on the south-east coast of Spain, bordering with the provinces of Granada and Murcia, with its coast lying between Costa Blanca and Costa del Sol. Almeria city has a preserved Moorish heritage with a Moorish fortress and old gypsy quarter. Other monuments include the Alcazabar and the cathedral. There is a big local African population and this is apparent from some of the shops and restaurants here. Almeria is a wealthy area with a high cost of living so be prepared. One thing to note is that property is on the whole cheaper than on the Costa del Sol but the prices are expected to rise. The higher cost of living acts as a barrier to ownership. Hopefully with time the property prices and cost of living will harmonise with the rest of the Costa del Sol resulting in capital growth and a cheaper cost of living. The climate gets very hot in the summer, this being one of its main attractions. As a result the tourism sector is set to expand as well as the facilities. Several sport centres are being built to cater for the forthcoming 2005 games so inward investment is high. If you want to benefit from this then buy when it is currently cheap – like now!
Hot website:	http://www.almeria-turismo.org/

Estate Agents:	Name	Address	Tel	Web
	Alfos Promociones Inmobiliarios S.L.	Tony Buckland 5th Floor 62–65 Trafalgar Square London WC2N 5DY	0207 925 1661 Fax: 0207 925 1881	http://www. aifos.es/ Email:london@ aifos.com
	Almerisol	Avda. Mediterraneo 99, 04740 Roquetas de Mar Almeria	0034 950 333 680/Fax: 0034 950 333 680	Not disclosed
	Casas Almeria	Urb. Costa Fleming, 04600 Huercal Overa, Almeria	0034 636 101 208/Fax: 0034 950 134 434	Not disclosed
	Inversiones Cellton S.L.	Calle San Pedro 4 Bajo, El Contador Almeria	0034 950 413 441	http://www. spanishmed property.com email: cellton@ teleline.es
Letting Agents:	Name	Address	Tel	Web
	Procosona S.L.	Ctra, Estación, 7 Bajo, Albox Almeria	0034 950 431 680/Fax: 0034 950 431 680	http://www. procosona.com email: info@ procosona.com
	Cristinas	C/Ramon y Cajal 9-local2 Almeria	0034 627 283 204/Fax: 0034 950 633 123	spanishhomes 8@hotmail.com
	Almeria In The Sun	Jose Jerez, Cabrera Sales Office, Cortijo Cabrera, Aptdo. Correos 17, Almeria	01708 721 919/ 01708 374 467	enquiries@ almeriain thesun.com
	Mediterra Inmobiliaria	Dársena 1, Local 3 Pto. Deportivo, Almerimar, 04700, El Ejido, Almería	Tel/Fax: 0034 950 497 960	http://www. mediterra spain.com/ email: info@ mediterra spain.com

Barcelona, Costa Brava					
Investor profile:	Worker, Business				
Category:	B				
Population:	Total 1.5 million			British 25,000	

Climate:	Hours of sunshine per day in summer	Days of rain per year	Average spring air temp.	Average summer air temp.	Average autumn air temp.	Average winter air temp.	Average water temp.
	9	96	13	24	16	10	18

Proximity to:	Airport 8 miles (Barcelona)	Beach 1 mile	Nearest city Barcelona
Educational facilities:	Number of universities 11	Number of international schools 6	Number of private schools 8
Health services:	Number of public hospitals 6	Number of private hospitals 4	Number of private clinics 12

Shopping:	Number of shopping centres 28	Number of markets 45
Restaurants and bars:	Wide choice of restaurants and bars, offering huge variety of different cuisines. Also local Catalan food available.	
Sports and leisure facilities:	Public sports centres with indoor swimming pools. Private sports clubs. 9-hole and 18-hole golf courses. Barcelona Football Club. Barcelona Royal Tennis Club. Picasso museum and other art museums. Cinemas. Theatres. Opera and ballet performances at Liceu Theatre. Jazz festival in November. Flamenco shows. Casino.12 nightclubs. Tibidabo Hill Amusement Park. A sea-life aquarium. Zoo. Port Aventura Theme Park (1.5 hour drive). Heron City leisure centre with shops, restaurants, cinemas and amusement arcades. Maremagnum leisure and residential complex with restaurants and cafes. Also several green areas within the city, including the main Parc de la Ciutadella.	

Transport:	Public transport Underground train (metro) service with 5 lines. Old-style trams (Tramvia Bleu) and cable cars from Montjuic to harbour. Mainline train services provide links to the suburbs. Trains also run to France, Eastern Spain and Madrid from Estacio de Francia train station. Regular bus services also within and around the city. Bus Turistic is a special tourist bus operating in Summer.	Roads N-II and E-15 from Girona. N-340 from Tarragona. A-2 from Zaragoza. A-7 from Valencia. N-II from Madrid.

Crime rate:	Low				
Main types of employment:	Business and manufacturing.				
Future plans:	AVE-high speed train link from Madrid (2004) 9 new skyscrapers built international cultural event Forum 2004.				
Yield range:	14.5%–17.0%				
Type of property:	Entry price	Rent – school holiday peak	Rent – peak	Rent – off peak	Average annual yield
2 bed apartment	200,000	1,495	1,196	718	17.0%
3 bed apartment	250,000	1,794	1,435	861	16.4%
3 bed townhouse	375,000	2,392	1,914	1,148	14.5%
Villa	440,000	3,140	2,512	1,507	16.3%
Demand for letting	School Holiday Peak High		Peak High		Off peak High
Finance and leisure scores:	Financial (out of 5) 4		Leisure (out of 5) 4		Total (out of 10) 8
Flights scheduled from:	Gatwick, Heathrow, London City, Luton, Stansted, Bristol, Cardiff, Newquay, Plymouth, Southampton, Birmingham, East Midlands, Humberside, Newcastle, Teesside, Isle of Man, Liverpool, Manchester, Aberdeen, Edinburgh, Glasgow, Inverness, Belfast City, Belfast International, Cork, Dublin, Guernsey, Jersey, Norwich, Leeds/Bradford.				
Typical cost of flights:	School holiday peak £171–282		Peak £127–209		Off peak £95–157
Operators:	Air Europa, BA, Iberia, Al Italia, Air France, Swiss Airlines, My Travel, Air2000, Easyjet, Thomas Cook.				
Description:	Barcelona is one of Spain's largest and liveliest cities, located on the north-east coast between the Costa Dorada and the Costa Brava. It is the capital of the Catalunia region and is Spain's most successful commercial centre, with a wealth of cultural and leisure activities. It is characterised by Gothic and Art Nouveau architecture, and also a large port. Tourist areas include the Antoni Gaudi monuments, the Sagrada Familia cathedral, the old Gothic cathedral (Barri Gotic), and Las Ramblas. The city has received much recognition since hosting the Olympics in 1992. The Olympics also led to new parks and gardens being built along the seafront. There is also now a promenade with shops and hotels along the 3-mile stretch of beach from Barceloneta to the riu Besos. Property in the city itself is generally expensive, although cheap properties can still be found in the old quarter. Popular places for foreign homebuyers to buy to live are the residential areas of Pedralbes, Sarria and Tres Torres located in the north of Barcelona, and Les Corts in the west of the city. Another desirable area is Vila Olympica by the port where there are modern apartments. Properties in the city centre mainly consist of apartments. Townhouses and villas are mainly found in the north and west of the city.				

Hot website:	http://www.bcn.es/english/ihome.htm			
Estate Agents:	**Name**	**Address**	**Tel**	**Web**
	John Taylor Real Estate Luxury Property Barcelona	Travessera de Gràcia, 1, Pral. 1a, 08021 Barcelona	0034 932 413 082 0034 932 413 088	http://www. johntaylorspain. com/index.html info@john taylorspain.com
	Olive Tree Investments	116 Furness Rd London	07973 513 724/Fax: 07980 685 445	email: nietoraf@ aol.com
	Barcelona Relocation Services	Calle Ganduxer 14, entl. 54, 08021 Barcelona	0034 932 034 935/Fax: 0034 932 401 577	Not disclosed
	Mundo Agencia	Calle San Hermenegildo, Local 24, 08006 Barcelona	0034 934 174 079/Fax: 0034 934 172 937	Not disclosed
Letting Agents:	**Name**	**Address**	**Tel**	**Web**
	John Taylor Real Estate Luxury Property Barcelona	Travessera de Gràcia, 1, Pral. 1a, 08021 Barcelona	0034 932 413 082 0034 932 413 088	http://www. johntaylorspain. com/index.html info@john taylorspain.com
	Fincas Corral	Gran Via de Les Corts Catalanes, 461 Barcelona	0034 934 241 450/Fax: 0034 934 260 529	http://www. fincascorral.com email: europa@ fincascorral.es
	Lançois-Doval	Passeig de Gràcia, 21, 1er Barcelona	0034 902 153 971	http://www. lancoisdoval.es email: ld@ lancoisdoval.es
	VillaRosa Estates	67–69 St Johns Road Waterloo Liverpool L22 9QB	0151 280 4027 Fax: 0151 280 5383	http://www. villarosaestates. com/ email: info@ villarosaestates. com

Benalmadena, Costa del Sol		
Investor profile:	Retirement, Worker, Holiday, Business	
Category:	A	

Population:	Total 36,000	British 2,000

Climate:	Hours of sunshine per day in summer	Days of rain per year	Average spring air temp.	Average summer air temp.	Average autumn air temp.	Average winter air temp.	Average water temp.
	11	45	21	28	24	16	20

Proximity to:	Airport 8 miles (Malaga)	Beach 0.25 miles	Nearest city 11 miles (Malaga)

Educational facilities:	Number of universities	Number of international schools	Number of private schools
	0	2	1

Health services:	Number of public hospitals	Number of private hospitals	Number of private clinics
	0	0	3

Shopping:	Number of shopping centres	Number of markets
	1	0

Restaurants and bars:	Most choice of international cuisine in Puerto Marina area. Bars in Puerto Marina and around 24-hour plaza. Several fast food outlets around Benalmadena Costa.

Sports and leisure facilities:	Private tennis and sports clubs. Golf courses. Public sports centre in Benalmadena village. Tivoli World theme park (near Arroyo de la Miel) offering rides, and concerts/cabaret shows at weekends. Cable car over mountains and above coast. Sealife marine centre and Selwo marine park. Casino at hotel Torrequebrada (Benalmadena Costa). Nightclubs at The Plaza/'24-hour square' and Puerto Marina.

Transport:	**Public transport** Train from Malaga or Fuengirola to Arroyo de la Miel. Bus services to Arroyo and Puerto Marina.	**Roads** N-340/A-7 from Costa del Sol. A-4 motorway from Madrid-Bailen-Jaen-Granada-Malaga-Benalmadena.

Crime rate:	Low.
Main types of employment:	Mainly tourist sector.
Future plans:	New residential area north of Benalmadena, with townhouses and some apartments and villas.
Yield range:	9.5%–11.1%

Type of property:	Entry price	Rent – school holiday peak	Rent – peak	Rent – off peak	Average annual yield
2 bed apartment	133,500	652	522	313	11.1%
3 bed apartment	166,875	782	626	376	10.7%
3 bed townhouse	250,313	1,043	835	501	9.5%
Villa	293,700	1,369	1,095	657	10.6%

Demand for letting:	School holiday peak High	Peak Medium	Off peak Low

Finance and leisure scores:	Financial (out of 5) 4	Leisure (out of 5) 4	Total (out of 10) 8

Flights scheduled from:	Gatwick, Heathrow, London City, Luton, Stansted, Bristol, Cardiff, Exeter, Newquay, Plymouth, Bournemouth, Southampton, Birmingham, East Midlands, Humberside, Newcastle, Teesside, Blackpool, Isle of Man, Liverpool, Manchester, Aberdeen, Edinburgh, Glasgow, Inverness, Belfast City, Belfast International, Derry, Cork, Dublin, Guernsey, Jersey, Norwich, Leeds/Bradford.

Typical cost of flights:	School holiday peak £201–320	Peak £149–237	Off peak £112–178

Operators:	Monarch, Swiss International, BA, Air France, Excel Airways, Futura, Thomas Cook, Astraeus, Air 2000, My Travel, Easyjet.

Description:	Benalmadena is one of the newer resorts on the coast, but has already become the second most popular tourist destination in the area (after Torremolinos). It consists of a tradional Andalucian village on a mountain, a 9 km coastal area (known as Benalmadena Costa), and the area between the two (called Arroyo de la Miel).

Benalmadena village is the quietest area. Arroyo de la Miel is busier and more commercialised, having the town's railway station, as well as many shops, businesses and accommodation. Benalmadena Costa is made up of big hotels and apartment blocks, and has a marina (called Puerto Marina). The marina has a hypermarket/small shopping centre and several restaurants, bars and nightclubs.

The area has just got its first Casino which is very upmarket and attracts clientele accordingly. There are still parts of it being built and when completed this resort will become one of Spain's finest. The climate here in the summer gets beyond hot! If you like a resort where you can get an instant tan then you won't be disappointed with Benalmadena.

Yields are above average and the potential for growth is above average so this makes it a true hotspot. Try to go no more than 0.25 miles inland to ensure your purchase rents out consistently. If you can, avoid holidaying during school peak as rental rates jump up here more than usual.

Hot website:	http://www.benalmadena.com/

Estate Agents:	Name	Address	Tel	Web
	Costa Del Sol Online Properties S.L.	Avda. de la Constitucion 37, Edificio Gavilan nº 9, Arroyo de la Miel, 29631 Benalmádena	0034 952 563 021/Fax: 0034 952 575 464	http://www.find ahomeinspain. com email: info@ findahome inspain.com
	Goulbourn Associates	Edf. Ins. Avda, Gamonal, Benalmadena Costa, Malaga 29630	0034 952 567 649/Fax: 0034 952 567 6 50	http://www. goulbourn associates.com/ email: info@ goulbourn associates.com
	Riviera Estates	Riviera del Sol El saladito 1 Bajo 6, 29649 Mijas Costa (Malaga)	0034 952 932 681 – 0034 952 935 160	http://www. rivieraestate spain.net/ miguel@riviera estatespain.net
	Spanish Living Group S.A.	Calle Lanzarote 2, Edifico Lorca 2 H, 29631 Arroyo de la Miel Malaga	0034 952 564 079/Fax: 0034 952 564 695	
Letting Agents:	Name	Address	Tel	Web
	Costa Del Sol Online Properties S.L.	Avda. de la Constitucion 37, Edificio Gavilan nº 9, Arroyo de la Miel, 29631 Benalmádena	0034 952 563 021/Fax: 0034 952 575 464	http://www.find ahomeinspain. com email: info@ findahome inspain.com
	Goulbourn Associates	Edf. Ins. Avda, Gamonal, Benalmadena Costa, Malaga 29630	0034 952 567 649/Fax: 0034 952 567 650	http://www. goulbourn associates.com/ email: info@ goulbourn associates.com
	Riviera Estates	Riviera del Sol El saladito 1 Bajo 6, 29649 Mijas Costa (Malaga)	0034 952 932 681 Fax: 0034 952 935 160	http://www. rivieraestate spain.net/ miguel@rivier aestatespain. net

Benidorm, Costa Blanca						
Investor profile:	Retirement, Worker, Holiday, Business					
Category:	A					
Population:	Total 56,500				British 3,000	
Climate:	Hours of sunshine per day in summer	Days of rain per year	Average spring air temp.	Average summer air temp.	Average autumn air temp.	Average winter air temp.	Average water temp.
	11	42	21	30	24	17	18
Proximity to:	Airport 31 miles (Alicante)		Beach 0.25 miles		Nearest city 24 miles (Alicante)	
Educational facilities:	Number of universities		Number of international schools		Number of private schools	
	1		0		3	
Health services:	Number of public hospitals		Number of private hospitals		Number of private clinics	
	1		1		30	
Shopping:	Number of shopping centres			Number of markets		
	2			1		
Restaurants and bars:	Predominantly fast food.					
Sports and leisure facilities:	Marina. Tennis clubs. Bowling clubs. Go-karting activities. Athletics track. Open-air concerts and theatre performances in amphitheatre. Terra Mitica theme park. Seaworld marine park. Aqualandia water park open in Summer. Nightclubs. 10 multi-screen cinemas, one showing English films weekly. Free jazz and classical concerts provided by council.					
Transport:	Public transport Frequent bus services within the town and to surrounding areas.			Roads N-332 from Valencia and Alicante.		
Crime rate:	Medium					
Main types of employment:	Mainly tourist sector, particularly in Summer season. High abundance of foreign companies in area.					
Future plans:	More residential and hotel complexes around Terra Mitica theme park.					
Yield range:	6.7%–7.5%					

Type of property:	Entry price	Rent – school holiday peak	Rent – peak	Rent – off peak	Average annual yield
2 bed apartment	218,181	670	536	322	7.0%
3 bed apartment	261,818	804	643	386	7.0%
3 bed townhouse	327,272	1,072	858	515	7.5%
Villa	480,000	1,407	1,126	675	6.7%

Demand for letting:	School holiday peak High	Peak High	Off peak High

Finance and leisure scores:	Financial (out of 5) 4	Leisure (out of 5) 5	Total (out of 10) 9

Flights scheduled from:	Gatwick, Heathrow, London City, Luton, Stansted, Bristol, Cardiff, Exeter, Newquay, Plymouth, Bournemouth, Southampton, Birmingham, East Midlands, Humberside, Newcastle, Teesside, Blackpool, Isle of Man, Liverpool, Manchester, Aberdeen, Edinburgh, Glasgow, Inverness, Belfast City, Belfast International, Derry, Cork, Dublin, Guernsey, Jersey, Norwich, Leeds/Bradford.

Typical cost of flights:	School holiday peak £192–485	Peak £142–359	Off peak £107–269

Operators:	Monarch, Iberia, BA, BMI, Air-Berlin, Thomas Cook, Easyjet, Flybe, Excel Airways, Britannia Airways, Futura, European Air Charter, My Travel, Astraeus, Air2000.

Description:	One of the oldest resorts in Spain, Benidorm is extremely well-developed and is Spain's biggest and busiest tourist resort. Mass tourism since the 1960's has led to many high-rise hotel and apartment blocks being built to form a new town. More recently there have been more green areas built in an attempt to improve its image. Benidorm has 2 main areas: the old town, with its traditional fishing port, and the new town, where the main resort lies. Benidorm has many visitors all year round. The 2 crescent-shaped main beaches stretched over 4 miles are Levante and Poniente. Benidorm is very lively with a huge abundance of nightlife. It is the busiest resort in Costa Blanca and demand for rental properties is consistent. The season runs all year round so simply owning a property here to make money is possible. If you're looking for an apartment then go for one as close as you can to the beach. You'll have rental competition from other landlords and being near the beach makes yours more attractive.

Hot website:	http://www.benidorm.to/

Estate Agents:	Name	Address	Tel	Web
	Paul Condron	Calle Gerona 39, 03503 Benidorm, Alicante	0034 965 654 272/Fax: 0034 646 339 825	Not disclosed
	Visual Home	Avda. Jaime I, 52, Local 7, Benidorm Alicante	0034 965 858 000	http://www.visual-home.com email: visual homes@tpi.infomail.es
	Limon Express	Estacion del Tren Benidorm	0034 966 803 103	email: limon expres@ telefonica.net
	Haart	P.O. Box 5995 Colchester Essex CO3 3WR	0845 600 7778	http://www.tmxhaart.co.uk/ email: webmaster @haart.co.uk
Letting Agents:	**Name**	**Address**	**Tel**	**Web**
	Costa Blanca Rentals	Suite 173, Ctra La Nao 71 03730 Javea	0034 966 460 681 Fax: 0034 966 460 681	http://www.cberentals.com email: info@ cberentals.com
	EuroCasa Gestion Inmobiliaria	Aptdo. Correos 2053 Alicante	0034 655 169 971	email: daniel combret@ yahoo.es
	Sajonia	Avda. Alfonso el Sabio 16, 8-Izq Alicante	0034 965 230 627 Fax: 0034 965 230 627	email: sajonia 21@yahoo.es
	ServiCasa	C/ Azorin 4, Bajo Alicante	0034 965 105 735/Fax: 0034 965 110 5601	http://www.interpisos.com/servicasa email: servicasa3 @hotmail.com

Blanes, Costa Brava		
Investor profile:	Retirement, Worker, Holiday, Business	
Category:	A	
Population:	Total 30,700	British 2,000
Climate:	Hours of sunshine per day in summer / Days of rain per year / Average spring air temp. / Average summer air temp. / Average autumn air temp. / Average winter air temp. / Average water temp. 9 96 21 28 24 15 19	
Proximity to:	Airport 17.5 miles (Girona)	Beach 0.25 miles	Nearest city 17.5 miles (Girona)
Educational facilities:	Number of universities 0	Number of international schools 0	Number of private schools 0
Health services:	Number of public hospitals 1	Number of private hospitals 0	Number of private clinics 2
Shopping:	Number of shopping centres 1	Number of markets 4	
Restaurants and bars:	Nearly 100 restaurants, including Catalan, Dutch, French, German, Mexican and other international cuisine.	
Sports and leisure facilities:	Martial arts clubs. 4 gyms. Tennis clubs. Water-skiing, windsurfing and parasailing courses. Calella south of Blanes annually holds Calella Activa – sport and cultural activities during summer, and a beer festival in October. Nearby Marineland complex with dolphin shows. Botanical gardens. Casino between Blanes and Lloret de Mar.	
Transport:	**Public transport** Train service from Barcelona every 30 minutes and Portbou. Trains run every 30 minutes to Barcelona and every 2 hours to Girona.	**Roads** A-19 and A-7 motorways from Barcelona to Blanes. N-II motorway from inland to Blanes. Palamos to Blanes along the coast.
Crime rate:	Medium	
Main types of employment:	Low unemployment rates in Catalonia.	
Future plans:	None	

Yield range:	19.0%–22.2%				
Type of property:	Entry price	Rent – school holiday peak	Rent – peak	Rent – off peak	Average annual yield
2 bed apartment	97,400	950	760	456	22.2%
3 bed apartment	121,750	1,140	912	547	21.3%
3 bed townhouse	182,625	1,520	1,216	730	19.0%
Villa	214,280	1,995	1,596	958	21.2%

Demand for letting:	School holiday peak High	Peak High	Off peak Low
Finance and leisure scores:	Financial (out of 5) 3	Leisure (out of 5) 5	Total (out of 10) 8

Flights scheduled from:	Gatwick, Heathrow, Luton, Stansted, Bristol, Cardiff, Newquay, Plymouth, Birmingham, East Midlands, Newcastle, Teesside, Isle of Man, Manchester, Aberdeen, Edinburgh, Glasgow, Inverness, Belfast City, Belfast International, Guernsey, Jersey, Leeds/Bradford.

Typical cost of flights:	School holiday peak £100–383	Peak £74–284	Off peak £56–213

Operators:	BA, Iberia, Air2000, Thomas Cook, Britannia Airways, My Travel.

Description:	Located on the most southern part of Costa Brava at the foot of Mount St. Joan, Blanes is a holiday resort particularly popular with Spanish holidaymakers of all ages.

Important monuments in the area include Saint Joan tower, Vescomtes de Cabrera church and El Vilar chapel. Blanes has a range of amenities, including 4 km of shingle beaches and a commercial centre with all the shops you need. The resort combines these modern facilities with the traditional feel of a Mediterranean fishing town. There is the Cuban Habaneras Festival (folksong concerts) during summer and the annual firework contest in July.

Property is considered cheap, and there has been an increase in the number of foreign purchasers. Captial growth is very likely as the only way is up! Many of the residential developments are set in pine forests. As a bonus the cost of living is also cheap, although it does increase in the Summer – but you cant have everything!

Hot website:	http://www.blanes.net/english

Estate Agents:	Name	Address	Tel	Web
	The Prestige Property Group	No Address	01935 817188 Fax: 01935 817199	http://www. prestigeproperty. co.uk email: sales@ prestigeproperty. co.uk

Estate Agents:	Name	Address	Tel	Web
	Fincas Fusté	A.P.I. nº453 Carrer Colom, 14 17300 Blanes	0034 972 354 536/Fax: 0034 972 354 518	http://www. fuste.com/ english/eng blanes.htm email: soniafc@ teleline.es
	Casa del Mar	8 Portland Place, Pritchard Street, Bristol, BS2 8RH	0870 429 4827/Fax: 0870 429 4828	Not disclosed
	DLR Properties Overseas	5 Manor Parade, Brightlingsea, Colchester, Essex CO7 0UD	01206 303 049 Fax: 01206 306 090	Not disclosed
Letting Agents:	Name	Address	Tel	Web
	Tossa de Mar	C/ Capità Mestres s/n Tossa de Mar Gerona	0034 972 342 815/Fax: 0034 972 342 641	http://www. tossa-de-mar. com email: Info@ Tossa-de- Mar.com

Caleta de Fuste, Fuerteventura

Investor profile:	Retirement, Worker, Holiday, Business		
Category:	A		

Population:	Total 52,500	British 2,000

Climate:	Hours of sunshine per day in summer	Days of rain per year	Average spring air temp.	Average summer air temp.	Average autumn air temp.	Average winter air temp.	Average water temp.
	11	41	22	26	25	20	20

Proximity to:	Airport 4 miles (Fuerteventura)	Beach 0.25 miles	Nearest city 8 miles (Puerto del Rosario)

Educational facilities:	Number of universities	Number of international schools	Number of private schools
	0	0	0

Health services:	Number of public hospitals	Number of private hospitals	Number of private clinics
	0	0	2

Shopping:	Number of shopping centres	Number of markets
	1	1

Restaurants and bars:	Variety serving both local and international cuisine.
Sports and leisure facilities:	Mostly water-sports – windsurfing, surfing, sailing, scuba-diving. Also deep-sea fishing opportunities. Tennis clubs. Horse-riding. Jeep safari. Kite surfing. Off road motorbiking. 18 hole golf course. Corralejo National Park. Catamaran excursions (dolphin and whale watching).

Transport:	**Public transport** Frequent bus service to Puerto del Rosario and other main towns on the island. No rail system.	**Roads** Motorway from Puerto del Rosario and Jandia peninsula in the south.

Crime rate:	Low
Main types of employment:	Mostly tourist sector – bars, restaurants.
Future plans:	Public hospital at Puerto del Rosario. Improvement of roads on Jandia Peninsula (south coast).
Yield range:	13.4%–15.0%

Type of property:	Entry price	Rent – school holiday peak	Rent – peak	Rent – off peak	Average annual yield
2 bed apartment	123,318	759	607	364	14.0%
3 bed apartment	147,981	911	729	437	14.0%
3 bed townhouse	184,977	1,214	972	583	15.0%
Villa	271,300	1,594	1,275	765	13.4%

Demand for letting:	School holiday peak High		Peak High		Off peak High

Finance and leisure scores:	Financial (out of 5) 5	Leisure (out of 5) 5	Total (out of 10) 10

Flights scheduled from:	Gatwick, Heathrow, Luton, Stansted, Bristol, Cardiff, Newquay, Plymouth, Bournemouth, Birmingham, East Midlands, Humberside, Newcastle, Teesside, Blackpool, Isle of Man, Liverpool, Manchester, Aberdeen, Edinburgh, Glasgow, Inverness, Belfast City, Belfast International, Dublin, Shannon, Guernsey, Jersey, Leeds/Bradford.

Typical cost of flights:	School holiday peak £315–806	Peak £233–597	Off peak £175–448

Operators:	Iberia, BA, SpanAir, Air Europa, Monarch, Thomas Cook, My Travel, Air 2000, Excel Airways, Britannia Airways, Astraeus, LTE International.

Description:	Caleta de Fuste is a modern and developing resort situated on the east coast, south of the capital Puerto del Rosario. The resort is set in a wide bay and is particularly favoured by families and couples. Fuerteventura is the second largest of the Canary Islands and is also one of the sunniest and hottest of the islands. Although resorts can be noisy and busy, the island in general is relatively undeveloped, so it is possible to have a relaxing and peaceful holiday. There are many holiday home developments in Caleta de Fuste. As the area is currently still quite undeveloped there is room for capital appreciation. The property market is currently growing at a rate of 20% per year. There is high demand for new properties and prices are rising. Rental rates are quite healthy so yields are too. I've given this area 10 out 10 as it has all the facilities and the potential profits!

Hot website:	http://www.fuerteventura.com/

Estate Agents:	Name	Address	Tel	Web
	Sunway Fuerteventura	Local Commercial 4, Virgen de Antigua, Poligono 22, 35600 Caleta de Fuste Antigua, Fuerteventura	0034 928 163 757/Fax: 0034 928 163 811	Not disclosed

Estate Agents:	Name	Address	Tel	Web
	Horizon Property Group S.L.	Local 14, Calle Isaac Peray, Esquina Garcia Morato, Corralejo 35660 Fuerteventura	0034 928 537 464/Fax: 0034 928 537 437	http://www. horizonproperty group.com/ fuerteventura/ email: info@ horizon- fuerteventura. com
	Select Resorts Ltd	2nd Floor 6 Old Generator House, Bourne Valley Road Poole, Dorset BH12 1DZ	01202 786 490 Fax: 01202 763 615	http://www. selectresorts. co.uk/ email: mail@ selectresorts. co.uk
	Freedom 4 Sale Spain	Antigua Sala de Proyeccion, Antigua Cine de Teguise, Calle Notes 15, Teguise 35530, Lanzarote	0034 928 845 944/Fax: 0034 928 845 936	http://www. freedom4sale. com/
Letting Agents:	**Name**	**Address**	**Tel**	**Web**
	Horizon Property Group S.L.	Local 14, Calle Isaac Peray, Esquina Garcia Morato, Corralejo 35660 Fuerteventura	0034 928 537 464/Fax: 0034 928 537 437	http://www. horizonproperty group.com/ fuerteventura/ email: info@ horizon- fuerteventura. com
	Secret Fuerteventura	Not disclosed	0034 928 538 477/Mobile: 647 561 057 Fax: 0034 928 868 578	email: lesley green@terra.es

Cadiz, Costa de la Luz

Investor profile:	Retirement, Worker, Holiday, Business		
Category:	B		
Population:	**Total** 140,000		**British** 2,000

Climate:	Hours of sunshine per day in summer	Days of rain per year	Average spring air temp.	Average summer air temp.	Average autumn air temp.	Average winter air temp.	Average water temp.
	11	108	20	29	21	16	14

Proximity to:	Airport 19 miles (Jerez)	Beach 0.5 miles	Nearest city Cadiz
Educational facilities:	Number of universities 1	Number of international schools 2	Number of private schools 5
Health services:	Number of public hospitals 1	Number of private hospitals 0	Number of private clinics 3

Shopping:	Number of shopping centres 0	Number of markets 2

Restaurants and bars:	Mostly Spanish cuisine, specialising in seafood such as lobster and prawns. Italian, Chinese and fast food also available.
Sports and leisure facilities:	4 watersports clubs. Real Tennis Club. Nearby Donana National Park – Europe's largest nature reserve. Fine arts and archaeological museum. Parque Groves outdoor theatre.

Transport:	**Public transport** Frequent bus services to Algeciras (12 daily), Jerez (every hour), Seville (11 daily), Almeria (2 daily), Granada (2 daily) and Malaga (6 daily). Train services to Jerez (20 daily), Seville (12 daily) and Granada (3 daily).	**Roads** N-340 from Estepona and Sotogrande. A-4 and N-IV motorway from Seville. N-IV from Cordoba.

Crime rate:	Low.
Main types of employment:	Shipping industry.
Future plans:	Many new developments under construction on coast. Regeneration of port. N-340 from single to dual carriageway 2005.
Yield range:	12.7%–14.9%

Type of property:	Entry price	Rent – school holiday peak	Rent – peak	Rent – off peak	Average annual yield
2 bed apartment	106,980	698	558	335	14.9%
3 bed apartment	133,725	838	670	402	14.3%
3 bed townhouse	200,588	1,117	893	536	12.7%
Villa	235,356	1,466	1,173	704	14.2%

Demand for letting:	School holiday peak Medium	Peak High	Off peak High

Finance and leisure scores:	Financial (out of 5) 5	Leisure (out of 5) 2	Total (out of 10) 7

Flights scheduled from:	Gatwick, Heathrow, Bristol, Newquay, Plymouth, Birmingham, Newcastle, Manchester, Leeds/Bradford, Aberdeen, Edinburgh, Glasgow, Inverness, Belfast City, Guernsey, Jersey.

Typical cost of flights:	School holiday peak £203–1,301	Peak £217–964	Off peak £163–723

Operators:	BA, Britannia Airways, Thomas Cook.

Description:	Cadiz is located on the south-western tip of mainland Spain. It has a large port and is more of a cosmopolitan rather than a typically Andalusian city. It has a low cost of living and demand for long term lets is high. This area is not a resort but considered more like a city close to the coast. This area should strongly appeal to the worker type investor. The main beach is Playa de la Caleta, but Playa de la Victoria is cleaner and has more sports facilities. Cadiz is popular with foreign buyers and residents. The old part of the city is surrounded by 18th century walls and has narrow streets full of tall 18th century houses and squares. Monuments include Cadiz Gothic cathedral and Torre Tavira baroque-style tower. Yields are healthy and are expected to be in the future. Don't expect any significant capital growth as there is no news of any major inward investment – but don't let this put you off. A nice income stream can be had from a long term let. If you plough all the profits back in to repaying the mortgage then the property could be yours within 7 years. After that the rent is all profit!

Hot website:	http://www.andalucia.com/cities/cadiz.htm

Estate Agents:	Name	Address	Tel	Web
	Secret Spain	Avda. Holanda 72, Roche Residential, 11149 Conil de la Fra, Cadiz	0208 551 5405 Fax: 0208 551 0760	Not disclosed

Estate Agents:	Name	Address	Tel	Web
	Realty Cádiz S.L.	Plaza España 3 Oficina 2 Cádiz	0034 606 700 640 Fax: 0034 956 536 390	http://www.realtycadiz.com email: info@realtycadiz.com
	Castlemain-Spain	Rinconada 13 Aloha Nueva Andalucia Marbella	0034 650 932 932/Fax: 0034 952 886 305	email: mail@casiro.com
	Inmo Chiclana Real Estate	Plaza España, Edificio España 3º, Oficina, 2 Chiclana de la Frontera	0034 606 700 640/Fax: 0034 956 536 390	http://www.inmochiclana.com email: sales@inmochiclana.com
Letting Agents:	**Name**	**Address**	**Tel**	**Web**
	Costa Holidays Vacation Rentals	Apartado de Correos 138 29680 Estepona Málaga	Not disclosed	http://www.costaholidays.com email: welcome1 @costaholidays.com
	Owners Direct Holiday Rentals	Not disclosed	01372 722708 Fax: 01372 744417	email: advertise @ownersdirect.co.uk

Costa del Silencio, Tenerife

Investor profile:	Retirement, Worker, Holiday, Business
Category:	A

Population:	Total 4,110	British 400

Climate:	Hours of sunshine per day in summer	Days of rain per year	Average spring air temp.	Average summer air temp.	Average autumn air temp.	Average winter air temp.	Average water temp.
	11	33	21.5	27	24	20	21

Proximity to:	Airport 3 miles (Reina Sofia)	Beach 0.25 miles	Nearest city 45 miles (Santa Cruz)

Educational facilities:	Number of universities	Number of international schools	Number of private schools
	0	0	0

Health services:	Number of public hospitals	Number of private hospitals	Number of private clinics
	0	0	0

Shopping:	Number of shopping centres	Number of markets
	0	0

Restaurants and bars:	Many bars and restaurants. Mostly British and fast food in coastal resort areas.

Sports and leisure facilities:	Both 18-hole Golf Amarillo (Tenerife's oldest golf course) and 27-hole Golf del Sur golf courses are championship courses. Bowls club. Tennis clubs. There are also residential complexes, shops, restaurants and sports clubs around each golf course. Windsurfing at El Medano – water sports village west of the resort.

Transport:	Public transport Frequent bus services (run by TITSA) to Playa de las Americas.	Roads Motorways from Santa Cruz.

Crime rate:	Low
Main types of employment:	Mainly tourist and service sectors. Many foreign companies based in and around the resort.
Future plans:	Second runway at Reina Sofia airport. New cinema complex.
Yield range:	13.4%–15.8%

Type of property:	Entry price	Rent – school holiday peak	Rent – peak	Rent – off peak	Average annual yield
2 bed apartment	101,143	699	559	336	15.8%
3 bed apartment	126,429	839	671	403	15.1%
3 bed townhouse	189,643	1,118	895	537	13.4%
Villa	222,515	1,468	1,174	705	15.0%

Demand for letting:	School holiday peak High	Peak High	Off peak Medium

Finance and leisure scores:	Financial (out of 5) 5	Leisure (out of 5) 4	Total (out of 10) 9

Flights scheduled from:	Gatwick, Heathrow, London City, Luton, Stansted, Bristol, Cardiff, Exeter, Newquay, Plymouth, Bournemouth, Southampton, Birmingham, East Midlands, Humberside, Newcastle, Teesside, Blackpool, Isle of Man, Liverpool, Manchester, Aberdeen, Edinburgh, Glasgow, Inverness, Prestwick, Belfast City, Belfast International, Dublin, Guernsey, Jersey, Norwich, Leeds/Bradford.

Typical cost of flights:	School holiday peak £154–464	Peak £114–344	Off peak £86–258

Operators:	Monarch, Iberia, Air Europa, BA, BMI, Flyjet, Air2000, Thomas Cook, Astraeus, Britannia Airways, LTE International, My Travel, Excel Airways, Futura.

Description:	Located on the south coast, Costa del Silencio is quieter than other resorts in Tenerife and is popular with people and families seeking a peaceful retreat. It is a purpose-built resort, has a small pebble beach and is close to the small fishing community of Las Galletas.

It's one of Tenerife's unsung resorts but it won't be for long! Prices are cheaper in this area compared to the rest of Tenerife hence the yields are well above average. The seasonal demand for property tails off in the off-peak season but demand still exists. If you require all year round occupation then make sure your property is better than the rest so it appeals more to prospective tenants.

It's easily accessible from the UK as there are many direct flights to the local airport which is only 3 miles away. There will be a second runway added to the airport to cater for the extra demand expected for this and surrounding areas. There is a shortage of homes being re-sold as people want to hold on to what they've got! If you can find a property with sea views that yields 12% or greater then buy it!

Hot website:	http://www.eurosol.com/

Estate Agents:	Name	Address	Tel	Web
	Freedom 4 Sale Spain	Antigua Sala de Proyeccion, Antigua Cine de Teguise, Calle Notes 15, Teguise 35530, Lanzarote	0034 928 845 944/Fax: 0034 928 845 936	http://www. freedom4sale. com/
	The Prestige Property Group	No Address	01935 817 188 Fax: 01935 817 199	http://www. prestige property.co.uk email: sales@ prestige property.co.uk
	The Horizon Property Group S.L.	Not disclosed Manchester	0161 476 0666 01384 866000	http://www. horizonproperty group.com/
	Eurosol	First Link CC Teide, Local 5 San Eugenio Alto Adeje 38660 Tenerife	0034 922 715 661/Fax: 0034 922 715 953	http://www. eurosol.com/
Letting Agents:	Name	Address	Tel	Web
	Eurosol	First Link CC Teide, Local 5 San Eugenio Alto Adeje 38660 Tenerife	0034 922 715 661/Fax: 0034 922 715 953	http://www. eurosol.com/
	Astliz Estate Agents	P.O.Box 135 Los Gigantes 38683 Santiago del Teide S/C de Tenerife	0034 922 796 776/Fax: 0034 922 796 973	http://www. canaryislands- internet.com/ email: info@ canarian-villas. com

Estepona, Costa del Sol		
Investor profile:	Retirement, Worker, Holiday, Business	
Category:	B	

Population:	Total 47,000	British 4,000

Climate:	Hours of sunshine per day in summer	Days of rain per year	Average spring air temp.	Average summer air temp.	Average autumn air temp.	Average winter air temp.	Average water temp.
	11	45	21	28	24	16	20

Proximity to:	Airport 46 miles (Malaga)	Beach 0.25 miles	Nearest city 49 miles (Malaga)

Educational facilities:	Number of universities	Number of international schools	Number of private schools
	0	1	0

Health services:	Number of public hospitals	Number of private hospitals	Number of private clinics
	0	0	3

Shopping:	Number of shopping centres	Number of markets
	2	1

Restaurants and bars:	More than 100 restaurants serve a variety of foods (including Andalusian, French, Chinese, Italian, and Indian), particularly around the town centre and port. Village of Benahavis known for its excellent food. Also good selection of British food. Karaoke bars.	

Sports and leisure facilities:	Sailing and water sports available in marina. 4 golf courses. Water skiing and parascending. Sub-aqua diving at diving centre at Atalaya Park Golf Hotel and Resort, which also has a sporting club and beach. Tennis and squash. Equestrian centre. Cycling and walking. Hunting and sport fishing. Art exhibitions and live music concerts in the town. Small cinema showing Spanish films. 4 nightclubs.	

Transport:	**Public transport** Regular bus service every 30 minutes on N-340 to rest of Costa del Sol. Daily bus service to Madrid and cities in Andalucia.	**Roads** A-7 motorway link to Algeciras. M-557 to Serrania de Ronda, then 333 Algeciras – Ronda provincial road.
Crime rate:	Low	
Main types of employment:	Tourist and service sectors. Knowledge of Spanish valuable.	
Future plans:	Widening of nearby N-340 motorway from single to dual carriageway (2004).	

Yield range:	7.2%–8.5%				
Type of property:	Entry price	Rent – school holiday peak	Rent – peak	Rent – off peak	Average annual yield
2 bed apartment	175,000	651	521	312	8.5%
3 bed apartment	218,750	781	625	375	8.1%
3 bed townhouse	328,125	1,042	833	500	7.2%
Villa	385,000	1,367	1,094	656	8.1%
Demand for letting:	School holiday peak High		Peak High		Off peak High
Finance and leisure scores:	Financial (out of 5) 2		Leisure (out of 5) 4		Total (out of 10) 6
Flights scheduled from:	Gatwick, Heathrow, London City, Luton, Stansted, Bristol, Cardiff, Exeter, Newquay, Plymouth, Bournemouth, Southampton, Birmingham, East Midlands, Humberside, Newcastle, Teesside, Blackpool, Isle of Man, Liverpool, Manchester, Aberdeen, Edinburgh, Glasgow, Inverness, Belfast City, Belfast International, Derry, Cork, Dublin, Guernsey, Jersey, Norwich, Leeds/Bradford.				
Typical cost of flights:	School holiday peak £201–320		Peak £149–237		Off peak £112–178
Operators:	Monarch, Swiss International, BA, Air France, Excel Airways, Futura, Thomas Cook, Astraeus, Air 2000, My Travel, Easyjet.				
Description:	Estepona is a medium-sized town and is a seaside resort offering more than 30 km of sandy beaches. It is less developed than other coastal resorts so is relatively more tranquil with large surrounding areas of unspoilt countryside – retaining a more 'Spanish' character.

It is located on the far west side of the coast and there are mountain villages that surround the town. Although traditionally a peaceful resort, it is becoming more popular, particularly with golfers. Sights to see include the clock tower, Los Remedios church, traditional old houses and castle remains. There are a number of high streets which mainly consist of fashion boutiques and leather stores. Festivities include carnival week (second week of February) and a fiesta on the 15th of May. Gibraltar is a 45 minute drive from Estepona.

There is a constant shortage of rental properties in Estepona, especially town houses and villas for long term lets. This has driven up the price of town house and villas due to the business investors moving in. But there are still some to be had and you'll have no problem letting them.

Estepona is one of the hottest resorts and the season is almost all year round. Rental demand is consistent throughout the year and will be in the future. Yields will be stable for at least the next 5 years. There is no sign of major capital growth within this time but over the long term it will move in line with the average. | | | | |
| Hot website: | http://www.pgb.es/estepona/ | | | | |

Estate Agents:	Name	Address	Tel:	Web
	Ate Consulting Financiero Inmobiliario	C/ San Francisco, 4 29670, San Pedro de Alcántara	0034 952 789 112/Fax: 0034 952 785 421	http://www.ate con.com/eng/ email: info@ atecon.com
	Bazan	C/Martínez Castro,s/n. Avenida de España, Edifico Jardin 29680 Estepona	0034 952 794 317/ Fax: 0034 952 794 317	http://www. wcostasol.es/ negocios/bazan /indice.htm Email. bazan@ wcostasol.es
	Gilmar – Consulting Inmobiliario	C/ Avda. Ricardo Soriano, 56 29600 Marbella (Málaga)	0034 952 861 341/Fax: 0034 952 827 386	http://gilmar realestate.com/ index.html email: gilmar@ gilmarrealestate. com
	Haciendas Garcia Navarro	Avda. Juan Carlos I, Bloque 2 bajo 29680 Estepona (Málaga)	0034 952 800 468/Fax: 0034 952 795 613	http://www. haciendas-garcia.com/ email: agencia @haciendas-garcia.com
Letting Agents:	Name	Address	Tel	Web
	Golden Mile Residences	Centro Comercial Guadalmina II, Ofic. 2 Guadalmina Alta, 29670 Marbella (Málaga)	0034 902 118 308/Fax: 0034 902 118 307	http://www. goldenmile.es/ email: info@ goldenmile.es
	Scandisol	A.P.I. Nº 622 C/ Santa Ana, 11 29680 Estepona (Málaga)	0034 952 771 736/Fax: 0034 952 823 461	http://www. scandisol.com/ english.htm email: estepona @scandisol.com
	Properties Select	Puerto Paraiso, Bl.7, Local 23 29680 Estepona (Málaga)	0034 952 808 613/806 477 Mob.: 0034 639 290 869 Fax: 0034 952 806 383 UK: 0871 222 8176	http://www. properties select.com/ email: john@ properties select.com
	Swan International	505 Pensby Road Thingwall Wirral CH61 7UQ	0034 952 888 296/Fax: 0034 952 883 800	http://www. swanint.co.uk/ Email. swanint @btinternet.com

Fuengirola, Costa del Sol

Investor profile:	Retirement, Worker, Holiday, Business
Category:	A

Population:	Total 55,000	British 7,000

Climate:	Hours of sunshine per day in summer	Days of rain per year	Average spring air temp.	Average summer air temp.	Average autumn air temp.	Average winter air temp.	Average water temp.
	11	45	21	28	24	16	20

Proximity to:	Airport 14 miles (Malaga)	Beach 0.25 miles	Nearest city 17 miles (Malaga)

Educational facilities:	Number of universities	Number of international schools	Number of private schools
	0	4	5

Health services:	Number of public hospitals	Number of private hospitals	Number of private clinics
	0	0	10

Shopping:	Number of shopping centres	Number of markets
	1	3

Restaurants and bars:	Most restaurants located around the old town behind the seafront. Specialist seafood restaurants can be found around San Francisco street in Los Boliches. Live music bars in town.

Sports and leisure facilities:	Public swimming and football clubs. 20 golf courses within a 30km radius of Fuengirola. Diving club. Private tennis clubs and gyms. A sailing club. Regular concerts and exhibitions in town at Casa de la Cultura. A theatre. A zoo. A marina with yachts and fishing boats. Sohail River Park – a 120,000 m² outdoor park and recreational area. Sohail castle (an Arab castle). Roman remains in town. 4 nightclubs. Festivities include Fuengirola fair in October and Feria del Carmen – a marine procession at Los Boliches in July.

Transport:	**Public transport** Train service between Malaga and Fuengirola. Bus service with several routes across the town. Bus service between town centre and Mijas aquatic park in Summer. Further bus services between town centre and Malaga, Marbella and Mijas.	**Roads** Directly situated on the N-340 motorway. The A-7 toll motorway also runs parallel from Fuengirola to Estepona (3 euros between Fuengirola and Marbella).

Crime rate:	Low

Main types of employment:	Mainly tourist and service sectors, particularly in the property market.				
Future plans:	Expansion along river to the north of Sohail castle, with new residential developments along with several hotels and large shopping complex. New road between town centre and new shopping centre. New car park beneath the church square. Re-development of port.				
Yield range:	9.0%–10.6%				
Type of property:	Entry price	Rent – school holiday peak	Rent – peak	Rent – off peak	Average annual yield
2 bed apartment	139,575	647	518	311	10.6%
3 bed apartment	174,469	776	621	373	10.1%
3 bed townhouse	261,703	1,035	828	497	9.0%
Villa	307,065	1,359	1,087	652	10.1%

Demand for letting:	School holiday peak High	Peak Medium	Off peak Low
Finance and leisure scores:	Financial (out of 5) 4	Leisure (out of 5) 5	Total (out of 10) 9

| Flights scheduled from: | Gatwick, Heathrow, London City, Luton, Stansted, Bristol, Cardiff, Exeter, Newquay, Plymouth, Bournemouth, Southampton, Birmingham, East Midlands, Humberside, Newcastle, Teesside, Blackpool, Isle of Man, Liverpool, Manchester, Aberdeen, Edinburgh, Glasgow, Inverness, Belfast City, Belfast International, Derry, Cork, Dublin, Guernsey, Jersey, Norwich, Leeds/Bradford. | | |

Typical cost of flights:	School holiday peak £201–320	Peak £149–237	Off peak £112–178

Operators:	Monarch, Swiss International, BA, Air France, Excel Airways, Futura, Thomas Cook, Astraeus, Air 2000, My Travel, Easyjet.
Description:	Fuengirola consists of over 5 miles of beaches with a promenade and is built up with many high rise apartment blocks and hotels. A popular tourist resort with holidaymakers of many different nationalities including the Spaniards themselves – so it can't be that bad! Although it has been extensively developed, a few traditionally Mediterranean-style buildings can still been found in the town e.g. the Pueblo Lopez neighbourhood. Fuengirola is one of the less expensive parts of the Costa del Sol to live, and during the winter season there are many residents of retired age. Small apartments are the cheapest type of property, while villas and townhouses particularly in Pueblo Lopez can be very expensive. Recently there have been new residential developments around the town, such as Las Lagunas, Los Pacos and Torreblanca – property here is often cheaper than Pueblo Lopez. Yields are healthy and above average but the growth prospects are even better. This place has loads of activities going on! Financially you can't go wrong with this area. It's easily accessible, not over priced, has low crime rates and is well connected.

Hot website:	www.fuengirola.org/			
Estate Agents:	**Name**	**Address**	**Tel**	**Web**
	SecondHouse InSpain	Avda. Jesus Santos Rein 74 Los Boliches Fuengirola Malaga	0034 606 537 855 Fax: 0034 952 667 469	www.Second HouseInSpain. com email: info@ secondhouse inspain.com
	Leiner Construimos Calidad	Avda. Los Boliches, 36 29640 Fuengirola	0034 952 667 213/Fax: 952 460 603	www.leiner.net email: Daniela@ leiner.net
	Leon Estates	C/ San Antonio, 15 29640 Fuengirola	0034 952 588 414 – 667 603 731/Fax: 952 663 363	www.leon estates.com email: info@ leonestates.com
	Venta de Propiedades	Avda. Los Boliches 109, Zona, Mercado, Los Boliches	0034 952 582 604 – 607 511 017/Fax: 952 582 318	www.inmobiliari avp.com email: ventaprop @ncs.es
Letting Agents:	**Name**	**Address**	**Tel**	**Web**
	Interealty	Avda. Alcalde Clemente Díaz Ruiz, Esq. San Juan de la Cruz, 29640 Fuengirola, Malaga	0034 952 665 081 Fax: 0034 952 665 159	www.interealty net.com email: infof@ interealtynet. com
	Leon Estates	C/ San Antonio, 15 29640 Fuengirola	0034 952 588 414 – 667 603 731/Fax: 0034 952 663 363	www.leon estates.com email: info@ leonestates.com
	Riviera Estates	Riviera del Sol El saladito 1 Bajo 6 29649 Mijas Costa (Malaga)	0034 952 932 681– 0034 952 935 160	www. rivieraestate spain.net/ email: miguel@ rivieraestate spain.net
	Gestion Inmobiliaria Joma	C/ San Pancracio Local 5 29640 Fuengirola	0034 952 584 414 – 667 603 731/Fax: 0034 495 258 414	www.inmobiliari ajoma.com email: info@ inmobiliari ajoma.com

Gandia, Costa Blanca

Investor profile:	Retirement, Worker, Holiday, Business
Category:	C

Population:	Total 59,850	British 2,000

Climate:	Hours of sunshine per day in summer	Days of rain per year	Average spring air temp.	Average summer air temp.	Average autumn air temp.	Average winter air temp.	Average water temp.
	11	42	21	30	24	17	18

Proximity to:	Airport 50 miles (Valencia)	Beach 0.25 miles	Nearest city 40 miles (Valencia)

Educational facilities:	Number of universities	Number of international schools	Number of private schools
	0	0	1

Health services:	Number of public hospitals	Number of private hospitals	Number of private clinics
	1	0	6

Shopping:	Number of shopping centres	Number of markets
	0	0

Restaurants and bars:	International and local cuisine.
Sports and leisure facilities:	18-hole golf course. Athletics track. International Classical Music Festival. Fishing port at Grau.

Transport:	**Public transport** 2 trains run daily between Gandía and Madrid during summer (only 1 daily in off-peak season). Trains every half an hour to Valencia all day, with connections to other cities.	**Roads** N-332 from Valencia and Benidorm. A-7 exit 60.

Crime rate:	Low
Main types of employment:	Predominantly tourist and service sectors.
Future plans:	None.
Yield range:	4.2%–4.7%

▶

Type of property:	Entry price	Rent – school holiday peak	Rent – peak	Rent – off peak	Average annual yield
2 bed apartment	208,636	401	321	192	4.4%
3 bed apartment	250,363	481	385	231	4.4%
3 bed townhouse	312,954	642	513	308	4.7%
Villa	459,000	842	674	404	4.2%

Demand for letting:	School holiday peak		Peak	Off peak
	High		High	Low

Finance and leisure scores:	Financial (out of 5)	Leisure (out of 5)	Total (out of 10)
	3	2	5

Flights scheduled from:	Gatwick, Heathrow, London City, Stansted, Bristol, Cardiff, Newquay, Plymouth, Southampton, Birmingham, Humberside, Newcastle, Teesside, Isle of Man, Manchester, Aberdeen, Edinburgh, Glasgow, Inverness, Belfast City, Belfast International, Guernsey, Jersey, Norwich, Leeds/Bradford.

Typical cost of flights:	School holiday peak	Peak	Off peak
	£174–296	£129–219	£97–164

Operators:	BA, Swiss International, Air France.

Description:	Part of the Marina Alta area in northern Costa Blanca, Gandia is a town situated at the foot of Safor mountain range. It has a port and beach, and also several monuments such as The Ducal Palace and Cathedral. The Gandia Playa coastal resort consists of over 4 miles of beaches alongside a palm-lined promenade.
	What sets this area apart from the others is that it has a rich feel to it. Property prices are expensive here but you do get a clean picturesque resort that seems to escape the hustle and bustle of its neighbours.
	Don't expect to make much of a return on your money. A purchase here is to enjoy your investment and hope for a return from capital growth. If you like what I like about this place then you'll be assured that someone else will 10 years down the line. The direction Spain is going any property bought in Spain will return above average returns. The more desirable area it is the more assured the gain will materialise.
	There are not that many operators that land in this area which can work for you. There isn't a heavy influx in or out of this area so the pace of the area is much slower than you would expect from a coastal Spanish resort.

Hot website:	http://www.abcgandia.com/en/index.html

Estate Agents:	Name	Address	Tel	Web
	Costa Azahar Homes	Plaza Mayor 9 Pta. 6, 46700 Gandia, Valencia	0034 962 872 805/Fax: 0034 962 864 285	Not disclosed

Estate Agents:	Name	Address	Tel	Web
	Property in Spain	10–16 Tiller Road London	0207 364 0500 Fax: 0207 364 0502	http://www.propertyin spain.net email: info@ propertyin spain.net
	Agencia Solmaran	Formentera 35 Playa de Gandia	0034 962 840 291	http:// www.solmaran.com email: api1152v @biapi.com
	Haart	P.O. Box 5995 Colchester Essex CO3 3WR	0845 600 7778	http://www.tmx haart.co.uk/ email: webmaster @ haart.co.uk
Letting Agents:	Name	Address	Tel	Web
	Costa Blanca Rentals	Suite 173, Ctra. La Nao 71 03730 Javea	0034 966 460 681/Fax: 0034 966 460 681	http://www.cberentals.com email: info@ cberentals.com
	EuroCasa Gestion Inmobiliaria	Aptdo. Correos 2053 Alicante	0034 655 169 971	email: daniel combret@ yahoo.es
	Sajonia	Avda. Alfonso el Sabio, 16, 8-Izq Alicante	0034 965 230 627 Fax: 0034 965 230 627	email: sajonia 21@yahoo.es
	ServiCasa	C/ Azorin, 4 – Bajo Alicante	0034 965 105 735/Fax: 0034 965 110 5601	http://www.interpisos. com/servicasa email: servicasa3 @hotmail.com

Ibiza Town, Ibiza

Investor profile:	Retirement, Worker, Holiday, Business
Category:	A

Population:	Total 34,800	British 2,500

Climate:	Hours of sunshine per day in summer	Days of rain per year	Average spring air temp.	Average summer air temp.	Average autumn air temp.	Average winter air temp.	Average water temp.
	11	40	15	25	20	12	17

Proximity to:	Airport 4.5 miles (Ibiza)	Beach 0.25–2 miles	Nearest city Ibiza Town (Eivissa)

Educational facilities:	Number of universities	Number of international schools	Number of private schools
	0	1	4

Health services:	Number of public hospitals	Number of private hospitals	Number of private clinics
	1	0	6

Shopping:	Number of shopping centres	Number of markets
	1	3

Restaurants and bars:	Wide selection of restaurants in Dalt Villa (old quarter), around marina/port, and along beaches. Many restaurants and bars close during off-peak season (late October to early May).
Sports and leisure facilities:	Casino complex with nightclub and restaurant at Passeig Maritim. Botafoch marina with yacht cruises. 4 further nightclubs – Pacha, El Divino, Angels and Anfora. Concerts, plays and recitals throughout the year. Expatriate theatre groups and sports clubs. Museum of Contemporary Art (in old town). Walking and hiking around rural villages further inland.

Transport:	Public transport Frequent bus services to San Antonio and Santa Eularia. Night bus (Discobus) between resort and main nightclubs during summer.	Roads Main roads from San Antonio and Sant Joan.

Crime rate:	High
Main types of employment:	Mostly tourist sector during Summer. Also salt trade.
Future plans:	New inner ring road to reduce congestion. Large auditorium.
Yield range:	13.3%–15.6%

Type of property:	Entry price	Rent – school holiday peak	Rent – peak	Rent – off peak	Average annual yield
2 bed apartment	247,888	1,700	1,360	816	15.6%
3 bed apartment	309,860	2,040	1,632	979	15.0%
3 bed townhouse	464,790	2,720	2,176	1,306	13.3%
Villa	545,354	3,570	2,856	1,714	14.9%

Demand for letting:	School holiday peak High	Peak High	Off peak Medium

Finance and leisure scores:	Financial (out of 5) 5	Leisure (out of 5) 5	Total (out of 10) 10

Flights scheduled from:	Gatwick, Heathrow, London City, Luton, Stansted, Bristol, Cardiff, Exeter, Newquay, Plymouth, Bournemouth, Southampton, Birmingham, East Midlands, Humberside, Newcastle, Teesside, Blackpool, Isle of Man, Liverpool, Manchester, Aberdeen, Edinburgh, Glasgow, Inverness, Prestwick, Belfast City, Belfast International, Dublin, Guernsey, Jersey, Norwich, Leeds/Bradford.

Typical cost of flights:	School holiday peak £282–1,025	Peak £209–759	Off peak £154–571

Operators:	SpanAir, Air Europa, Monarch, Air France, Britannia Airways, My travel, Astraeus, Iberworld, Thomas Cook, Air 2000, Excel Airways.

Description:	Ibiza Town is the capital of Ibiza, one of the Balearic Islands located 52 miles from the eastern Spanish coast. Although most of the island is unspoilt with rural architecture and olive groves, resorts such as Ibiza Town are very busy during peak season.

Most residents of Ibiza live in Ibiza Town. It is essentially an old town, the old quarter being known as 'Dalt Villa' with narrow cobbled streets, an old medieval castle, cathedral and stone walls. The three other main districts of the town are Puig des Molins (in the hills), Sa Penya (old fishing district), and Eixample (modern quarter).

The town has a large gay and hippy population, and this is reflected in the local markets. Like Majorca, property in Ibiza is relatively expensive, although prices are expected to continue rising. This does not surprise me as the rental yields are brilliant. It's only a matter of time before these yields are eroded away by the spiralling property prices. My advice to you is get in there quick!

One drawback of the area is that not only does Ibiza attract holidaymakers it also attracts the thieves! Ibiza is addressing this problem and there is now a stronger police presence. Spain understand that this island is the jewel in their crown and they will do whatever it takes to protect it.

Hot website:	http://www.ibiza-spotlight.com/

Estate Agents:	Name	Address	Tel	Web
	Fincas Eivissa	Carretera Ibiza San José Kilómetro 1,5 Apart Can Bellotera	0034 639 694 469/Fax: 0034 971 398 185	http://www. fincaseivissa. com/ email: fincas eivissa@inter book.net
	Interealty Balearics	Plaza Santa Ponsa, 4, Local 1 en E-07180, Santa Ponsa Mallorca	0034 971 699 545/Fax: 0034 971 699 556	www.interealty-mallorca.com
	Inmobiliaria Villa Contact	Paseo. S'Alamera 14, 07840 Santa Eulalia del Rio Ibiza	0034 971 330 374/331 554 Fax: 0034 971 330 458	http://www. villacontact. com/ email: info@ villacontact.com
	BBS Consulting Raimund Schreck-Heuer	Avda. Es Cubells 1, Edificio S'Atalaya, Bajos F Apdo. 164 E-07830 San José Ibiza	0034 971 800 705/Fax: 0034 971 800 664 Mob: 0034 649 190 465	http://www. bbs-ibiza.com/ eng/index_en. htm email: bbs@ctv. es
Letting Agents:	Name	Address	Tel	Web
	Houseland-co-ibiza	Unknown	0034 971 318 539	http://www. houseland-co-ibiza.com/ingles /principal.htm email: info@ house-co-ibiza.com

Granada, Andalusia		
Investor profile:	Retirement, Worker, Holiday, Business	
Category:	C	
Population:	**Total** 285,000	**British** 3,000

Climate:	Hours of sunshine per day in summer	Days of rain per year	Average spring air temp.	Average summer air temp.	Average autumn air temp.	Average winter air temp.	Average water temp.
	11	40	18	31	22	12	21

Proximity to:	Airport 7.5 miles (Granada)	Beach 80 miles	Nearest city Granada
Educational facilities:	Number of universities 1	Number of international schools 1	Number of private schools 4
Health services:	Number of public hospitals 4	Number of private hospitals 3	Number of private clinics 18

Shopping:	Number of shopping centres 1	Number of markets 2

Restaurants and bars:	Largely specialises in local cuisine, which has Arab influences. Seafood restaurants can be found on the coast. There is also a wide range of international food.	
Sports and leisure facilities:	18-hole golf course at Las Gabias. 11-hole golf course at Los Moriscos. Tennis club. Sierra Nevada skiing resort nearby. 2 water-parks on city outskirts open during summer. Music, theatre and dance festivals in summer. Science museum with planetarium and butterfly park. Archaelogical museum and art museum near Alhambra. Cinemas and theatres (Spanish language). Generalife gardens.	

Transport:	**Public transport** Bus routes between city centre and other parts of city. Also frequent bus services to Madrid, Malaga and Seville and to surrounding towns and villages. Train services to Malaga, Seville and Madrid.	**Roads** N-340 dual carriageway from Costa del Sol. A-92 from Seville. N-IV and N-323 from Madrid.
Crime rate:	Low	
Main types of employment:	Tourist sector and teaching of languages.	

▶

Future plans:	New second ring road around city. Dual carriageways from city to coast and to Almeria.				
Yield range:	3.9%–4.5%				
Type of property:	Entry price	Rent – school holiday peak	Rent – peak	Rent – off peak	Average annual yield
2 bed apartment	151,515	300	240	144	4.5%
3 bed apartment	189,394	360	288	173	4.3%
3 bed townhouse	284,091	480	384	230	3.9%
Villa	333,333	630	504	302	4.3%
Demand for letting:	School holiday peak Medium		Peak Medium		Off peak High
Finance and leisure scores:	Financial (out of 5) 2		Leisure (out of 5) 4		Total (out of 10) 6
Flights scheduled from:	Gatwick, Heathrow, Bristol, Newquay, Plymouth, Birmingham, Newcastle, Manchester, Leeds/Bradford, Aberdeen, Edinburgh, Glasgow, Inverness, Belfast City, Guernsey, Jersey.				
Typical cost of flights:	School holiday peak £286–491		Peak £212–364		Off peak £159–273
Operators:	Iberia, BA.				
Description:	Granada is located in eastern Andalusia, at the foot of the Sierra Nevada mountain range. It is essentially an historical city, and houses the Moorish palace known as the Alhambra which is Spain's most visited monument. Around the Alhambra is the Moorish quarter of Albaicin, a particular hotspot within the city, where property is highly desired. The houses are characterised by being set within cobbled stoned streets and they are all brilliant white in colour. There are many squares dotted within this area to relax and take in the views, including the Alhambra itself. Apart from the historical element, the city is also cosmopolitan with many tourists and university students. Property is in demand as there is a relative shortage of re-sale properties, although there has been much recent construction around the city's outskirts. Even so, prices are expected to continue rising. The holiday season, ironically, is quieter than other times. Because the students go home and others head to the resorts to relax on the beach. But the nightlife is by no way quiet! The are really only two sections which stay open late: 1. Pedro Alarcon which is for the 18–30 age range. 2. Plaza Nueva which is for the older crowd. There is an uprising of unofficial parties by the younger residents which, depending on how you feel, could be a good thing or a bad thing!				
Hot website:	http://granadainfo.com/english.htm				

Estate Agents:	Name	Address	Tel	Web
	Delta Service	Plaza Madrid 1, 18690 Granada, Almeria	0034 958 639 149/Fax: 0034 958 630 025	Not disclosed
	Edney & Barea S.L.	Doctor Sofre 1, 18850 Cullar, Granada, Almeria	0034 958 732 438/Mob: 0034 650 673 698	Not disclosed
	Wilkinson Estates	Cortijo del Zorro, Lista de Correos, 18740 Castell de Ferro, Granada	0034 958 349 238	Not disclosed
	Granada Estates	Avda. Jual Carlos I Almunecar Andalusia	Not disclosed	http://www. granada estates.com email: info@ granada estates.com
Letting Agents:	Name	Address	Tel	Web
	Wilkinson Estates	Cortijo del Zorro, Lista de Correos, 18740 Castell de Ferro, Granada	0034 958 349 238	Not disclosed
	Granada Estates	Avda. Jual Carlos I Almunecar Andalusia	Not disclosed	http://www. granada estates.com email: info@ granada estates.com

Islantilla, Costa de la Luz		
Investor profile:	Retirement, Worker, Holiday, Business	
Category:	C	
Population:	Total 2,500	British 100

Climate:	Hours of sunshine per day in summer	Days of rain per year	Average spring air temp.	Average summer air temp.	Average autumn air temp.	Average winter air temp.	Average water temp.
	11	108	20	29	21	16	18

Proximity to:	Airport 37.5 miles (Faro)	Beach 0.25 miles	Nearest city 24 miles (Huelva)
Educational facilities:	Number of universities 0	Number of international schools 0	Number of private schools 0
Health services:	Number of public hospitals 0	Number of private hospitals 1	Number of private clinics 2

Shopping:	Number of shopping centres 1	Number of markets 0

Restaurants and bars:	Good selection of bars and restaurants, particularly in neighbouring village of La Antilla.	
Sports and leisure facilities:	Islantilla International Golf Resort (27-hole) with 3 courses. Most other sport/leisure facilities e.g. swimming, tennis, are in hotels and resorts.	

Transport:	Public transport Limited bus services. Private transport recommended.	Roads E-1 from Seville. N-IV and E-1 from Cordoba. E-5/A-4 and A-49 from Cadiz.

Crime rate:	Low	
Main types of employment:	Mainly tourist and service sector.	
Future plans:	A relatively new resort, Islantilla continues to expand with new developments and amenities.	
Yield range:	7.2%–8.4%	

Type of property:	Entry price	Rent – school holiday peak	Rent – peak	Rent – off peak	Average annual yield
2 bed apartment	135,000	498	398	239	8.4%
3 bed apartment	168,750	598	478	287	8.1%
3 bed townhouse	253,125	797	637	382	7.2%
Villa	297,000	1,046	837	502	8.0%

Demand for letting:	School holiday peak High	Peak Medium	Off peak Low

Finance and leisure scores:	Financial (out of 5) 3	Leisure (out of 5) 3	Total (out of 10) 6

Flights scheduled from:	Gatwick, Heathrow, London City, Stansted, Bristol, Newquay, Plymouth, Southampton, Birmingham, East Midlands, Newcastle, Isle of Man, Manchester, Aberdeen, Edinburgh, Glasgow, Inverness, Belfast City, Belfast International, Cork, Dublin, Guernsey, Jersey, Leeds/Bradford.

Typical cost of flights:	School holiday peak £247–564	Peak £183–418	Off peak £137–314

Operators:	BA, Air Portugal, Iberia, Excel Airways, My Travel, Astraeus, Thomas Cook, Flyjet, Monarch, Air2000, Britannia.

Description:	Islantilla is a new tourist area recently developed, with a large golf resort, sandy beaches and promenade. It is situated on the south-western coast of the mainland, close to the border with Portugal and is a small, quiet resort. The busy fishing town of Isla Cristina and the city of Huelva are both close by. There are several white sandy beaches in this area which make the area very desirable. Another draw to this area is the 27-hole golf course.
	Capital growth is likely but not within 5 years. This is a long term investment punt. It's still being developed and has a long way to go but the right companies are moving in and if they are you should be too!
	If you buy here you know you can be in Portugal within an hour. So you can almost have the best of both worlds. Access is easy as many airports fly to Faro, the airport serving this area. The entry level price is just above £100k so it's not that cheap. Yields are affected accordingly and are therefore not that strong. The yields look sustainable however as price growth will not occur for a while. Yields may even increase over the short term depending on the popularity of the area.

Hot website:	http://www.islantillagolfresort.com/

Estate Agents:	Name	Address	Tel	Web
	Escape2.com Ltd.	Hamilton House, 205 Bury New Road, Whitefields, Manchester M45 6GE	0161 280 7375 Fax: 0191 959 5680	Not disclosed

Estate Agents:	Name	Address	Tel	Web
	Roger N Coupe-Spanish Property Sales	3 Bank Buildings, High Street, Cranleigh, Surrey GU6 8BB	01483 548 340 Fax: 01483 548 341	Not disclosed
	ACD Spanish Properties	125 Summerhouse Drive, Bexley, Kent DA5 2ER	01322 550 409 Fax: 01322 550 409	Not disclosed
	Beaches International Property Ltd.	3 & 4 Hagley Mews, Hagley Hall, Stourbridge, West Midlands DY9 9LQ	01562 885 181 Fax: 01562 886 724	Not disclosed
Letting Agents:	Name	Address	Tel	Web
	Holiday Accommodation Overseas Ltd.	2233 Coventry Road, Sheldon Birmingham B26 3EH	0871 781 1205	http://www.holiday-apartments.net/portugal-algarve-islantilla.htm

Javea, Costa Blanca

Investor profile:	Retirement, Worker, Holiday, Business		
Category:	C		

Population:	Total 28,000		British 5,600

Climate:	Hours of sunshine per day in summer	Days of rain per year	Average spring air temp.	Average summer air temp.	Average autumn air temp.	Average winter air temp.	Average water temp.
	11	42	21	30	24	17	18

Proximity to:	Airport 60 miles (Alicante)	Beach 0.25–1.2 miles	Nearest city 60 miles (Alicante)

Educational facilities:	Number of universities	Number of international schools	Number of private schools
	1	3	4

Health services:	Number of public hospitals	Number of private hospitals	Number of private clinics
	0	0	1

Shopping:	Number of shopping centres	Number of markets
	0	1

Restaurants and bars:	Local speciality is fish and seafood. Many fish restaurants found at Aduanas del Mar. International and local cuisine also available.
Sports and leisure facilities:	Children's play areas at Arenal beach. Large fishing port. Water sports e.g. scuba-diving, windsurfing in marina. Also sailing club in marina. Sporting Alfas Cricket Club. 9-hole golf course at Javea Golf Club. Bowling green. 3 tennis clubs. Bridge club. Horse-riding, netball and rugby clubs. Sant Antoni Marine Reserve. Montgo Natural Park. Cinema with English film once a week. English language theatre productions.

Transport:	Public transport Buses to Moraira, Gandia, Denia and Calpe.	Roads N-332 from Valencia, Alicante, Gandia and Benidorm. A-7 from Alicante, Barcelona and Valencia.

Crime rate:	Medium
Main types of employment:	Predominantly tourist and service sectors.
Future plans:	Improved road connections to surrounding region.
Yield range:	7.4%–8.7%

Type of property:	Entry price	Rent – school holiday peak	Rent – peak	Rent – off peak	Average annual yield
2 bed apartment	140,000	532	420	255	8.7%
3 bed apartment	175,000	638	511	306	8.3%
3 bed townhouse	262,500	851	681	409	7.4%
Villa	308,000	1,117	894	536	8.3%

Demand for letting:	School holiday peak High		Peak High		Off peak Low

Finance and leisure scores:	Financial (out of 5) 3	Leisure (out of 5) 3	Total (out of 10) 6

Flights scheduled from:	Gatwick, Heathrow, London City, Luton, Stansted, Bristol, Cardiff, Exeter, Newquay, Plymouth, Bournemouth, Southampton, Birmingham, East Midlands, Humberside, Newcastle, Teesside, Blackpool, Isle of Man, Liverpool, Manchester, Aberdeen, Edinburgh, Glasgow, Inverness, Belfast City, Belfast International, Derry, Cork, Dublin, Guernsey, Jersey, Norwich, Leeds/Bradford.

Typical cost of flights:	School holiday peak £192–485	Peak £142–359	Off peak £107–269

Operators:	Monarch, Iberia, BA, BMI, Air-Berlin, Thomas Cook, Easyjet, Flybe, Excel Airways, Britannia Airways, Futura, European Air Charter, My Travel, Astraeus, Air2000.

Description:	Situated in northern Costa Blanca in the Marina Alta region, Javea is a small historic town set around a sea port at the foot of Montgo mountain. The 3 main areas are: 1) The old town – traditional architecture and narrow streets; 2) Aduana del mar – the old fishermen's quarter on the coast by the marina and fishing port, and 3) El Arena – the main resort area with beaches. Javea is relatively quiet and is away from the main roads. It has 25 kms of coastline with 8 beaches including some pebble/rock beaches. The coastline also has caves and attractive, small coves. Sights to see in the old town include the Church of San Bartholeme. Property is expensive compared to the rest of the coast and the area is popular with foreign investors. The yields are okay but have been eroded a bit in the last 5 years due to the popularity of this area from these investors. It's still a good area however as capital growth is likely. This area appeals to the discerning investor wishing to combine holidaying with speculative investing.

Hot website:	http://www.javea-online.com/

Estate Agents:	Name	Address	Tel	Web
	Lambourne Properties	Calle Ronda 1, Colon, 03730 Javea, Alicante	0034 965 795 916/Fax: 0034 965 795 916	Not disclosed
	R M Inmobiliaria	Avda. Marina Espanola 13 bajo, 03730 Javea, Alicante	0034 966 461 939/Fax: 0034 965 795 299	Not disclosed
	Valuvillas.Com	Edificio Caribe 11, Avda. del Pla 129, 03730 Javea, Alicante	0034 966 462 244/Fax: 0034 965 795 060	Not disclosed
	Haart	P.O. Box 5995 Colchester Essex CO3 3WR	0845 600 7778	http://www.tmxhaart.co.uk/ email: webmaster@haart.co.uk
Letting Agents:	Name	Address	Tel	Web
	Costa Blanca Rentals	Suite 173, Ctra. La Nao 71 03730 Javea	0034 966 460 681/Fax: 0034 966 460 681	http://www.cberentals.com email: info@cberentals.com
	EuroCasa Gestion Inmobiliaria	Aptdo. Correos 2053 Alicante	0034 655 169 971	email: danielcombret@yahoo.es
	ServiCasa	C/ Azorin, 4 – Bajo Alicante	0034 965 105 735/Fax: 0034 9651 105 601	http://www.interpisos.com/servicasa email: servicasa3@hotmail.com

La Gomera, Canary Islands		
Investor profile:	Retirement, Worker, Holiday, Business	
Category:	C	
Population:	**Total** 18,000	**British** 700

Climate:	Hours of sunshine per day in summer	Days of rain per year	Average spring air temp.	Average summer air temp.	Average autumn air temp.	Average winter air temp.	Average water temp.
	9	38	23	27	26	22	21

Proximity to:	Airport 100 miles (La Palma)	Beach 0 miles	Nearest city 100 miles (Santa Cruz de Palma)
Educational facilities:	Number of universities 0	Number of international schools 0	Number of private schools 0
Health services:	Number of public hospitals 1	Number of private hospitals 1	Number of private clinics 5

Shopping:	Number of shopping centres 0	Number of markets 2
Restaurants and bars:	Local, Indian and Chinese food widely available. Most restaurants and bars concentrated around Valle Gran Rey resort.	
Sports and leisure facilities:	Water-based sports – windsurfing, sailing, scuba diving and fishing. Tecina 18-hole golf course. Mountain-hiking clubs. Cycling. The north of the island has old churches, mansions, exhibitions of traditional art and handiwork and island museum. De Garajonay national park. Nightlife mostly based within hotel complexes.	

Transport:	**Public transport** Limited bus service between main towns.	**Roads** Main road across island via National Park. Secondary roads around mountains.
Crime rate:	Low	
Main types of employment:	Agriculture, tourism.	
Future plans:	New marina at Valle Gran Rey. New golf course at Playa de Santiago.	
Yield range:	5.4%–6.3%	

Type of property:	Entry price	Rent – school holiday peak	Rent – peak	Rent – off peak	Average annual yield
2 bed apartment	180,000	497	398	239	6.3%
3 bed apartment	225,000	596	477	286	6.0%
3 bed townhouse	337,500	795	636	382	5.4%
Villa	396,000	1,044	835	501	6.0%

Demand for letting:	School holiday peak	Peak	Off peak
	High	High	High

Finance and leisure scores:	Financial (out of 5)	Leisure (out of 5)	Total (out of 10)
	3	4	7

Flights scheduled from:	Gatwick, Manchester.

Typical cost of flights:	School holiday peak	Peak	Off peak
	£360–1,138	£267–843	£200–632

Operators:	Iberia, BA.

Description:

La Gomera has one of the smallest populations among the Canary Islands thus is largely undeveloped and unspoilt. The island is very mountainous, forming lakes and waterfalls and valleys rich in water. There is also a variety of flora on the island e.g. fig trees, orange trees, cacti and over 100,000 palm trees.

The capital San Sebastian de Gomera is the island's main port and is an historic town famous for being the departure point of Christopher Columbus in 1492. Directly opposite the capital lies the developing resort of Valle Gran Rey, which is proving to be more and more popular each year. The resort has many coffee shops along the sea front – the perfect place to relax and look over the ocean (with a trained eye you can see Tenerife)! Look out for Hermigua where you can buy all the crafts produced by this Island to send back as gifts to your friends and family.

There are few flights to this Island, only available from two UK airports, but this can be a good thing if you want a quieter life in Spain. You can get to La Gomera by taking a flight to Tenerife and then a ferry. This can work out a lot cheaper!

There is a high demand for property as future construction is limited. Prices are expected to rise over the next few years due to the lack of supply. If you are looking for a quiet holiday home that you can rent out during the off-peak seasons then La Gomera could be the place. It has high demand all the year through and generally your tenants will be of an older age so the risk of damage is minimal.

Hot website:	http://www.1stcanaryislands.com/lagomera.shtml

Estate Agents:	Name	Address	Tel	Web
	DLR Properties Overseas	5 Manor Parade, Brightlingsea, Colchester, Essex CO7 0UD	01206 303 049 Fax: 01206 306 090	Not disclosed

Estate Agents:	Name	Address	Tel	Web
	Yes Property International	Legend House, 10 Market Place, Faversham, Kent ME13 7AG	0870 300 4260	Not disclosed
	Haart	P.O. Box 5995 Colchester Essex CO3 3WR	0845 600 7778	http://www.tmx haart.co.uk/ email: webmaster@ haart.co.uk
	Canarias Estates	Avda. Tirajana 37, Ed. Mercurio 2, 7C, 35100 Playa del Ingles, Gran Canaria	0034 928 761 159/Fax: 0034 928 776 992	http://www. canariasestates. com/ email: canesta@ terra.es
Letting Agents:	Name	Address	Tel	Web
	Realizaciones Inmobiliarias Canarias, S.A.	Avda. Jablillo, s/n Teguise Address not known	0034 928 590 296	Not disclosed

La Manga, Costa Blanca

Investor profile:	Retirement, Worker, Holiday, Business
Category:	A

Population:	Total 50,000		British 2,000

Climate:	Hours of sunshine per day in summer	Days of rain per year	Average spring air temp.	Average summer air temp.	Average autumn air temp.	Average winter air temp.	Average water temp.
	11	42	21	30	24	17	18

Proximity to:	Airport 15 miles (Murcia)	Beach 0.25 miles	Nearest city 15 miles (Murcia)

Educational facilities:	Number of universities	Number of international schools	Number of private schools
	0	1	0

Health services:	Number of public hospitals	Number of private hospitals	Number of private clinics
	1	1	5

Shopping:	Number of shopping centres	Number of markets
	4	0

Restaurants and bars:	Local, Italian, Indian and Chinese restaurants on Mediterranean side of La Manga. Local cuisine and tapas bars on Mar Menor side. Excellent choice of local and Spanish cuisine in nearby village of Cabo de Palos.
Sports and leisure facilities:	4 marinas offering variety of water sports including scuba-diving. 12 sailing schools. 3 golf courses at Club La Manga Resort. Horse riding. Tennis clubs. Hiking and mountaineering at Cartegena Sierra. Casino. Specialised local mud spas. 3 open-air cinemas showing Spanish films throughout Summer. San Pedro del Pinatar Regional Park (about 1,750 acres of wild land, in the north of urbanized La Manga), Calblanque Regional Park (about 6,200 acres of wild land, craggy cliffs above sand beaches, south of La Manga).

Transport:	**Public transport** Restricted. Private transport recommended.	**Roads** N-301 from Murcia. A-7 and A-37 from Valencia and Costa Blanca.

Crime rate:	Medium
Main types of employment:	Tourist work during Summer only.
Future plans:	Restricted amount of area left in La Manga, so future developments e.g. new golf courses and residential complexes in other parts of the Mar Menor area.

Yield range:	16.9%–18.9%				
Type of property:	Entry price	Rent – school holiday peak	Rent – peak	Rent – off peak	Average annual yield
2 bed apartment	78,181	606	485	291	17.7%
3 bed apartment	93,818	727	582	349	17.7%
3 bed townhouse	117,272	970	776	465	18.9%
Villa	172,000	1,273	1,018	611	16.9%
Demand for letting:	School holiday peak High		Peak Medium		Off peak Low
Finance and leisure scores:	Financial (out of 5) 5		Leisure (out of 5) 4		Total (out of 10) 9
Flights scheduled from:	Gatwick, Heathrow, London City, Stansted, Bristol, Newquay, Plymouth, Southampton, Birmingham, East Midlands, Newcastle, Isle of Man, Manchester, Aberdeen, Edinburgh, Glasgow, Inverness, Belfast City, Belfast International, Cork, Dublin, Guernsey, Jersey, Leeds/Bradford.				
Typical cost of flights:	School holiday peak £266–803		Peak £197–595		Off peak £148–446
Operators:	Iberia, Air Europa, Astraeus, GB Airways, BMI, BA, Planet Air, Flybe, Ryanair, My Travel.				

Description:	La Manga is a 13 mile-long narrow section of land located between Mar Menor – the largest saltwater lake in Europe – and the Mediterranean Sea.
	    It has many high-rise hotels and apartment blocks – more than half the amount in the whole of Murcia. A large number of tourists visit during Summer making it a popular resort. Most property is located on the beach-front. The western end of the strip has mostly apartments and hotels, while the eastern end is quieter and more residential, with many townhouses and villas.
	    For some reason this area is undervalued. You can get a 2 bed apartment for less than £50k! Yields are fantastic even though the off-peak season has low demand. If you can manage to let it out through the peak periods you will cover all costs of ownership. There is a shortage of villas in this area so investment in one of these will ensure a high occupancy rate.
	    There is plenty to do here and there always will be. This area is one of the most established resorts in Costa Blanca. Not only will this be a safe investment due to the attraction for tenants of its facilities, it will be a fun place to have a holiday home as there is so much to do.				

Hot website:	http://www.lamangaspain.com/				

Estate Agents:	Name	Address	Tel	Web
	Xanadu Property Mart	Lo Pagan, Mar Menor, Murcia	0034 965 329 025	http://www. xanaduproperty mart.co.uk email: chrisof laherty2002@ yahoo.co.uk
	Haart	P.O. Box 5995 Colchester Essex CO3 3WR	0845 600 7778	http://www. tmxhaart.co.uk/ email: web master@haart. co.uk
	Select Resorts Ltd	2nd Floor 6 Old Generator House, Bourne Valley Road Poole, Dorset BH12 1DZ	01202 786 490 Fax: 01202 763 615	http://www. selectresorts. co.uk/ email: mail@ selectresorts. co.uk
Letting Agents:	**Name**	**Address**	**Tel**	**Web**
	Marítima Inmobiliaria	Mopu building, Mediterranean Sea side, Gran Vía de la Manga Km. 0	0034 968 146 170/Fax: 0034 968 564 254	email: maritima 2001@jazzfree. com
	Inmobiliaria Los Arcos	Centro Comercial Mangamar, Gran Vía de la Manga Km. 0 330380 La Manga del Mar Menor (Murcia)	0034 968 564 111/Fax: 0034 968 337 318	email: inmo losarcos@ inmolosarcos. com
	Rent In Manga	Miramar Urbanization, Km. 0,4 Gran Vía de La Manga, Mar Menor side	0034 968 563 279	Not disclosed
	Apartamentos Dos Mares	Gran Vía de La Manga, Km. 3, corner Plaza Bohemia, Dos Mares building	0034 968 140 096/Fax: 0034 968 140 137	email: mangazul @mx3.redestb.es

La Palma, Canary Islands

Investor profile:	Retirement, Worker, Holiday, Business		
Category:	C		
Population:	Total 80,000		British 2,000

Climate:	Hours of sunshine per day in summer	Days of rain per year	Average spring air temp.	Average summer air temp.	Average autumn air temp.	Average winter air temp.	Average water temp.
	11.5	88	22	25	26	21	21

Proximity to:	Airport Santa Cruz La Palma	Beach 0 miles	Nearest city Santa Cruz
Educational facilities:	Number of universities 0	Number of international schools 0	Number of private schools 1
Health services:	Number of public hospitals 1	Number of private hospitals 1	Number of private clinics 6

Shopping:	Number of shopping centres 0	Number of markets 4

Restaurants and bars:	Local cuisine specialising in fish found in the capital Santa Cruz de la Palma. Also small selection of other foods.
Sports and leisure facilities:	Canary Islands Cultural Park. Maroparque zoo near Santa Cruz de la Palma. 4 scuba-diving centres. 3 horse-riding organisations. 6 mountain-biking clubs. Rock-climbing. Parasailing.Walking and hiking tours. Astrophysical observatory in 'El Roque de los Muchachos'. Palma Club flying tours. Marine tours.

Transport:	Public transport Bus services between main towns. Regular ferry services to Tenerife.	Roads 1 main road across the island via the national park. Secondary roads around mountains.

Crime rate:	Low
Main types of employment:	Agriculture, tourism.
Future plans:	New golf course at Los Llanos. New bridges between main towns. New tunnel from Brena Alta to El Paso. 2 new marinas at Santa Cruz and Tazacorte.
Yield range:	5.8%–6.8%

Type of property:	Entry price	Rent – school holiday peak	Rent – peak	Rent – off peak	Average annual yield
2 bed apartment	132,222	395	316	190	6.8%
3 bed apartment	165,278	474	379	228	6.5%
3 bed townhouse	247,916	632	506	303	5.8%
Villa	290,888	830	664	398	6.5%

Demand for letting:	School holiday peak	Peak	Off peak
	High	High	Medium

Finance and leisure scores:	Financial (out of 5)	Leisure (out of 5)	Total (out of 10)
	3	3	6

Flights scheduled from:	Gatwick, Manchester.		

Typical cost of flights:	School holiday peak £360–1138	Peak £267–843	Off peak £200–632

Operators:	Iberia, BA.		

Description:	La Palma is the fifth largest of the Canary Islands. It is triangular shaped with a varied landscape consisting of mountains, woodlands, black sandy bays and a volcanic crater (known as Caldera de Taburiente).
	La Palma is less developed than Tenerife, Gran Canaria and Lanzarote and most of it is unspoilt, including the capital Santa Cruz de la Palma. The capital is situated on the west coast, and has well-preserved colonial architecture. South of the capital is the quiet beach resort of Los Cancajos. In the south of the island is the lively resort of Fuencalienta de la Palma, and on the west of the island are the quieter resorts of Puerto de Tazacorte and Puerto Naos. Puerto Naos is renowned for its beach.
	There are few flights to this Island, only available from two UK airports, but this can be a good thing if you want a quieter life in Spain. You can get to La Palma by taking a flight to Tenerife and then a ferry. This can work out a lot cheaper!
	La Palma makes a perfect retirement home. It is quiet but still close enough to the buzz and commercialism of Tenerife, if required, by ferry and the property prices are not as high compared to the rest of the Islands. There is a high demand for property as construction is limited. Expect prices to rise as La Palma becomes more discovered by outsiders.

Hot website:	http://www.canary-travel.com/La_Palma/index-in.html

Estate Agents:	Name	Address	Tel	Web
	DLR Properties Overseas	5 Manor Parade, Brightlingsea, Colchester, Essex CO7 0UD	01206 303 049 Fax: 01206 306 090	Not disclosed

Estate Agents:	Name	Address	Tel	Web
	Yes Property International	Legend House, 10 Market Place, Faversham, Kent ME13 7AG	0870 300 4260	Not disclosed
	Haart	P.O. Box 5995 Colchester Essex CO3 3WR	0845 600 7778	http://www.tmx haart.co.uk/ email: webmaster@ haart.co.uk
	Canarias Estates	Avda. Tirajana 37, Ed. Mercurio 2, 7C, 35100 Playa del Ingles, Gran Canaria	0034 928 761 159/Fax: 0034 928 776 992	http://www. canariasestates. com/ email: canesta@ terra.es
Letting Agents:	Name	Address	Tel	Web
	Realizaciones Inmobiliarias Canarias, S.A.	Avda. Jablillo, s/n Teguise Address unknown	0034 928 590 296	Not disclosed

Las Palmas, Gran Canaria

Investor profile:	Retirement, Worker, Holiday, Business
Category:	B

Population:	Total	British
	350,000	20,000

Climate:	Hours of sunshine per day in summer	Days of rain per year	Average spring air temp.	Average summer air temp.	Average autumn air temp.	Average winter air temp.	Average water temp.
	11	63	24	26	24	21	20

Proximity to:	Airport	Beach	Nearest city
	17 miles (Las Palmas)	0.25 miles	Las Palmas

Educational facilities:	Number of universities	Number of international schools	Number of private schools
	1	3	3

Health services:	Number of public hospitals	Number of private hospitals	Number of private clinics
	4	5	7

Shopping:	Number of shopping centres	Number of markets
	2	1

Restaurants and bars:	International selection of bars and restaurants, as well as local cuisine.

Sports and leisure facilities:	2 marinas for sailing and other water sports. Cruising and yachting at Puerto de la Luz (also Europe's largest port). Sports complex with tennis, horse-riding and rock-climbing. 2 golf courses, including Real Club de Las Palmas – set on an extinct volcanic crater. Annual classical music and opera festivals during autumn. 2 casinos. An auditorium. Cinema complexes.

Transport:	Public transport	Roads
	UTINSA bus service to most of island.	Motorway to south along east coast. Motorways to Trasmontana and Tarifa Alta.

Crime rate:	Medium
Main types of employment:	Tourist and service industries.
Future plans:	None.
Yield range:	9.7%–11.4%

Type of property:	Entry price	Rent – school holiday peak	Rent – peak	Rent – off peak	Average annual yield
2 bed apartment	129,962	649	519	312	11.4%
3 bed apartment	162,453	779	623	374	10.9%
3 bed townhouse	243,679	1,038	831	498	9.7%
Villa	285,916	1,363	1,090	654	10.9%

Demand for letting:	School holiday peak High		Peak High		Off peak High

Finance and leisure scores:	Financial (out of 5) 4		Leisure (out of 5) 4		Total (out of 10) 8

Flights scheduled from:	Gatwick, Heathrow, London City, Luton, Stansted, Bristol, Cardiff, Exeter, Newquay, Plymouth, Bournemouth, Southampton, Birmingham, East Midlands, Humberside, Newcastle, Teesside, Blackpool, Isle of Man, Liverpool, Manchester, Aberdeen, Edinburgh, Glasgow, Inverness, Prestwick, Belfast City, Belfast International, Cork, Dublin, Shannon, Guernsey, Jersey, Norwich, Leeds/Bradford.

Typical cost of flights:	School holiday peak £286–1,278	Peak £212–947	Off peak £159–710

Operators:	Iberia, Air Europa, BA, SpanAir, Astraeus, My Travel, Britannia Airways, Air2000, Excel Airways, Monarch, Thomas Cook.

Description:	Las Palmas is the capital city of Gran Canaria (the 3rd largest Canary Island) and also the shopping capital of the islands. Every shop you need can be found here. It has a big city feel and the restaurants help to match that with cuisine from all around the world.

Description continued: One thing that is great about this part is that the public bus service is excellent. So if you're not a car driver but want to move to Spain then this city might be for you.

Despite the 3 million holidaymakers seeking sun shine and relaxation the island has maintained its rural, Mediterranean charm. Although it is no longer as popular as southern resorts, it has a large foreign population and is very cosmopolitan.

Its coastline is around 4 miles long. It also has an old quarter in the Vegueta and Triana districts in the south. Visitors numbers are consistent and therefore demand is consistent for rental properties. There isn't much development going on so your purchase is likely to be a re-sale property. The yields are slightly better than average so you can be assured that this area would be one of the safer investments.

Hot website:	http://www.gran-canaria-info.com/

Estate Agents:	Name	Address	Tel	Web
	Maherma S.A.	Pérez Galdós, 24-1º Las Palmas de Gran Canaria	0034 928 368 524/Fax: 0034 928 380 186	http://www. maherma.com/ email: maherma @maherma.com
	Esica	Mallorca, 13, 1º Izq. Los Tarahales Las Palmas de Gran Canaria	0034 928 412 654/Fax: 0034 928 421 237	http://www. viviendasen canarias.com/ gc/esica.htm email: esicanet @teleline.es
	Ofertas Inmobiliaria en Canarias	Avda. de las Tinajas, 23 Vecindario Las Palmas de Gran Canaria	0034 655 611 795	http:// viviendasen canarias.com email: viviendas @viviendasen canarias.com
	Freedom 4 Sale Spain	Antigua Sala de Proyeccion, Antigua Cine de Teguise, Calle Notes 15, Teguise 35530, Lanzarote	0034 928 845 944/Fax: 0034 928 845 936	http://www. freedom4sale. com/

Letting Agents:	Name	Address	Tel	Web
	Canarias Estates	Avda. Tirajana 37, Ed. Mercurio 2, 7C, 35100 Playa del Ingles, Gran Canaria	0034 928 761 159/Fax: 0034 928 776 992	http://www. canariasestates. com/ email: canesta@ terra.es
	Gestion Inmobiliaria Mercacentro	Victor Jara (C.C. Mercacentro) 35110 Vecindario Gran Canaria	Tel/Fax: 0034 928 758 111 Mob: 0034 639 216 866	http://www. inmobiliaria mercacentro .com/ email: merca- inmobiliaria@ terra.com
	RAO Estate	C/ Botánico, Local 57, 35100 San Fernando de Maspalomas Gran Canaria	0034 639 778 338/Fax: 0034 928 764 837	http://www. raoestate.com/ email: info@ raoestate.com
	Grupo Vesua, S.L.	C/ Drago, 48 Gáldar Gran Canaria	0034 928 897 105/Fax: 0034 928 551 153	http:// viviendasen canarias.com/ vesua/

Lloret de Mar, Costa Brava		
Investor profile:	Retirement, Worker, Holiday, Business	
Category:	A	
Population:	Total 20,000	British 1,000

Climate:	Hours of sunshine per day in summer	Days of rain per year	Average spring air temp.	Average summer air temp.	Average autumn air temp.	Average winter air temp.	Average water temp.
	9	96	21	27	20	15	19

Proximity to:	Airport 25 miles (Girona)	Beach 0.25 miles	Nearest city 27 miles (Girona)
Educational facilities:	Number of universities 0	Number of international schools 0	Number of private schools 6
Health services:	Number of public hospitals 0	Number of private hospitals 0	Number of private clinics 5

Shopping:	Number of shopping centres 7	Number of markets 4
Restaurants and bars:	International bars and restaurants including British, Chinese, Indonesian, German and Italian. Also fast food.	
Sports and leisure facilities:	Athletics track. Multisports pavilion (basketball, handball, table tennis, skating, judo, gymnastics and indoor football). Go-karting track. Tennis clubs. Parascending courses. Pleasure cruises. Horse-riding classes. 10-pin bowling. Mini-golf course. 18-hole golf club (Club de Golf Angel de Lloret) nearby. Sailing courses and boat hire at Fenals Maritime Club. Verdaguer Cultural Centre. Theme park with funfair rides. 20 Nightclubs. A casino. WaterWorld water-park open in Summer. Port Aventura theme park nearby. Aquatic zoo. Traditional dance shows at Placa de la Vila during peak season.	

Transport:	**Public transport** 7 bus operators in area offering service within area and to Barcelona and rest of Costa Brava. 4 train lines operate in area.	**Roads** Exit 9 off A-7 motorway, then C-63 to Lloret de Mar.
Crime rate:	Low	
Main types of employment:	Mostly service sector.	
Future plans:	None.	

Yield range:	21.6%–25.3%				
Type of property:	Entry price	Rent – school holiday peak	Rent – peak	Rent – off peak	Average annual yield
2 bed apartment	69,500	771	617	370	25.3%
3 bed apartment	86,875	925	740	444	24.3%
3 bed townhouse	130,313	1,234	987	592	21.6%
Villa	152,900	1,619	1,295	777	24.1%
Demand for letting:	School holiday peak High		Peak Medium		Off peak Low
Finance and leisure scores:	Financial (out of 5) 5		Leisure (out of 5) 4		Total (out of 10) 9
Flights scheduled from:	Gatwick, Heathrow, Luton, Stansted, Bristol, Cardiff, Newquay, Plymouth, Birmingham, East Midlands, Newcastle, Teesside, Isle of Man, Manchester, Aberdeen, Edinburgh, Glasgow, Inverness, Belfast City, Belfast International, Guernsey, Jersey, Leeds/Bradford.				
Typical cost of flights:	School holiday peak £100–383		Peak £74–284		Off peak £56–213
Operators:	BA, Iberia, Air2000, Thomas Cook, Britannia Airways, My Travel.				
Description:	A very developed self-contained resort consisting of many high-rise apartment and hotel blocks, popular with the British package tourists. It has 5 sand and shingle beaches, with a choice of services and leisure activities at each one. A promenade lined with palm trees has recently been added to make it more attractive. It is less crowded than Costa Blanca. The town of Lloret has a Gothic church and a 10th century chapel. Property prices are cheap, cheap, cheap! You can nick a 1 bed property here for around £30k. Not only that it's cheap to get here! Yields are fantastic and the scope for growth is excellent. This area is a low risk entry to Spain if you are seriously considering buying in Spain. There's loads to do here and if you only rent out the property in the school holiday peak then you'll cover all costs. That means you get a holiday home for free for the rest of the year – now that can't be bad!				
Hot website:	http://www.lloretguide.com				
Estate Agents:	Name	Address	Tel	Web	
	The Prestige Property Group	No Address	01935 817 188 Fax. 01935 817 199	http://www. prestigeproperty. co.uk email: sales@ prestigeproperty. co.uk	

▶

Estate Agents:	Name	Address	Tel	Web
	Directo Constructor	Carretera de Blanes 101 Lloret de Mar 17310-Girona	0034 972 360 615/Fax: 972 373 013	http://www. directo constructor.com/ en/empresa.asp email: info@ directo constructor.com
	European Estates	52 Portland Place, London W1B 1NH	0207 631 7940/Fax: 0207 631 7946	Not disclosed
	Hamptons International	168 Brompton Road, London SW3 1HW	Tel: 0207 589 3884/Fax: 0207 584 4365	Not disclosed
Letting Agents:	**Name**	**Address**	**Tel**	**Web**
	Tossa de Mar	C/ Capità Mestres s/n Tossa de Mar Gerona	0034 972 342 815/Fax: 0034 972 342 641	http://www. tossa-de-mar. com email: Info@ Tossa-de- Mar.com

Los Cristianos, Tenerife

Investor profile:	Retirement, Worker, Holiday, Business
Category:	B

Population:	Total	British
	2,960	300

Climate:	Hours of sunshine per day in summer	Days of rain per year	Average spring air temp.	Average summer air temp.	Average autumn air temp.	Average winter air temp.	Average water temp.
	11	33	21.5	27	24	20	21

Proximity to:	Airport	Beach	Nearest city
	11 miles (Reina Sofia)	0.25 miles	45 miles (Santa Cruz)

Educational facilities:	Number of universities	Number of international schools	Number of private schools
	0	1	2

Health services:	Number of public hospitals	Number of private hospitals	Number of private clinics
	1	0	1

Shopping:	Number of shopping centres	Number of markets
	0	1

Restaurants and bars:	A wealth of restaurants and bars, mainly concentrated around the harbour, including British, Italian, Chinese, seafood and local restaurants.
Sports and leisure facilities:	Scuba-diving courses, sailing and surfing in large marina. Public sports centre with indoor swimming pool. Own golf course with 3 other golf courses (Adeje, Los Palos and Amarilla Golf) nearby. Go-karting club with 3 different circuits. Tennis clubs. Cinema complex showing English-language films throughout the Summer. Ecological Park in Las Aguilas with 75,000 sq. metres of tropical gardens and a variety of wildlife, including crocodiles, penguins and elephants. Bananaera tropical gardens. Camel Park. Cactus and Animal Park.

Transport:	**Public transport** Frequent bus services (run by TITSA) across island's main roads.	**Roads** Motorways from Santa Cruz.

Crime rate:	Medium
Main types of employment:	Mainly tourist and service sectors. Many foreign companies based in and around the resort.
Future plans:	New cinema complex.
Yield range:	9.0%–10.5%

Type of property:	Entry price	Rent – school holiday peak	Rent – peak	Rent – off peak	Average annual yield
2 bed apartment	115,200	532	426	255	10.5%
3 bed apartment	144,000	638	511	306	10.1%
3 bed townhouse	216,000	851	681	409	9.0%
Villa	253,440	1,117	894	536	10.1%

Demand for letting:	School holiday peak High	Peak High	Off peak High

Finance and leisure scores:	Financial (out of 5) 4	Leisure (out of 5) 4	Total (out of 10) 8

Flights scheduled from:	Gatwick, Heathrow, London City, Luton, Stansted, Bristol, Cardiff, Exeter, Newquay, Plymouth, Bournemouth, Southampton, Birmingham, East Midlands, Humberside, Newcastle, Teesside, Blackpool, Isle of Man, Liverpool, Manchester, Aberdeen, Edinburgh, Glasgow, Inverness, Prestwick, Belfast City, Belfast International, Dublin, Guernsey, Jersey, Norwich, Leeds/Bradford.

Typical cost of flights:	School holiday peak £154–464	Peak £114–344	Off peak £86–258

Operators:	Monarch, Iberia, Air Europa, BA, BMI, Flyjet, Air2000, Thomas Cook, Astraeus, Britannia Airways, LTE International, My Travel, Excel Airways, Futura.

Description:	Los Cristianos is Tenerife's second largest resort. It is situated around a port and, unlike Playa de las Americas, developed from a fishing village. Although it is full of high-rise apartment complexes and large resorts, it still retains a trace of this old fishing town charm. There are 2 main beaches offering a variety of watersports and excursions. It is a popular place for owning a holiday home. The prices are not as attractive as other parts of Tenerife but you can be assured of an all year round let. The yields are reflected accordingly but the area still offers above average yields. Do not expect double digit capital growth figures because you won't get it. This part of Tenerife is already developed but what it will offer you is an excellent holiday home that will pay for itself and more!

Hot website:	http://www.eurosol.com/

Estate Agents:	Name	Address	Tel	Web
	The Horizon Property Group S.L.	Local no. 25, Centro Commercial Don Antonio, nº 19 Calle Juan XXIII, 38650 Los Cristianos, Arona, Tenerife	0034 922 792 651/Fax: 0034 922 795 319	Not disclosed

Estate Agents:	Name	Address	Tel	Web
	Tenerife Properties Direct	Prolongacion Avda. De Suecia, Edificio Guanapay Local No. 1, 38650 Los Cristianos, Arona, Tenerife	0034 922 796 636/Fax: 0034 922 796 647	Not disclosed
	Klein Immobilien	Avda. de Suecia 35 Los Cristianos Tenerife	0034 922 753 165/Fax: 0034 922 753 165	http://tenpro. net/ email: kleinimmo @arrakis.es
	Freedom 4 Sale Spain	Antigua Sala de Proyeccion, Antigua Cine de Teguise, Calle Notes 15, Teguise 35530, Lanzarote	0034 928 845 944/Fax: 0034 928 845 936	http://www. freedom4sale. com/
Letting Agents:	**Name**	**Address**	**Tel**	**Web**
	Eurosol	First Link CC Teide – Local 5 San Eugenio Alto Adeje 38660 Tenerife	0034 922 715 661/Fax: 0034 922 715 953	http://www. eurosol.com/
	Astliz Estate Agents	P.O. Box 135 Los Gigantes 38683 Santiago del Teide S/C de Tenerife Canary Islands	0034 922 796 776/Fax: 0034 922 796 973	http://www. canaryislands- internet.com/ email: info@ canarian-villas. com

Los Delfines, Menorca

Investor profile:	Retirement, Worker, Holiday, Business					
Category:	B					
Population:	Total 5,000				British 750	
Climate:	Hours of sunshine per day in summer	Days of rain per year	Average spring air temp.	Average summer air temp.	Average autumn air temp.	Average winter air temp.	Average water temp.
	11	65	20	27	23	13	17
Proximity to:	Airport 31.5 miles (Mahon)		Beach 0.25 miles		Nearest city 30 miles (Mahon)	
Educational facilities:	Number of universities 0		Number of international schools 0		Number of private schools 2	
Health services:	Number of public hospitals 0		Number of private hospitals 0		Number of private clinics 1	
Shopping:	Number of shopping centres 1			Number of markets 0		
Restaurants and bars:	The number of restaurants and bars is smaller than on other Balearic Islands, and many restaurants close in off-peak season. Lots of fast food available, particularly pizzerias.					
Sports and leisure facilities:	Small water park at Cala'n Forcat. Diving clubs. Nightclubs and bars open until midnight only.					
Transport:	Public transport Local bus service to Ciutadella every 20 minutes.		Roads One main road through centre of island between Mahon and Ciudadela.			
Crime rate:	Low					
Main types of employment:	Tourist sector during peak season. Limited number of foreign workers.					
Future plans:	Increased size of national parks and marine reserves.					
Yield range:	9.4%–11.0%					

Type of property:	Entry price	Rent – school holiday peak	Rent – peak	Rent – off peak	Average annual yield
2 bed apartment	189,300	910	728	437	11.0%
3 bed apartment	236,625	1,092	874	524	10.5%
3 bed townhouse	354,938	1,456	1,165	699	9.4%
Villa	416,460	1,911	1,529	917	10.5%

Demand for letting:	School holiday peak High		Peak Medium	Off peak Low

Finance and leisure scores:	Financial (out of 5) 3	Leisure (out of 5) 3	Total (out of 10) 6

Flights scheduled from:	Gatwick, Luton, Stansted, Bournemouth, Bristol, Cardiff, Birmingham, East Midlands, Manchester, Liverpool, Leeds/Bradford, Humberside, Teesside, Newcastle, Glasgow, Edinburgh.

Typical cost of flights:	School holiday peak £120–543	Peak £89–402	Off peak £67–302

Operators:	Monarch, Iberia, BA, My Travel, Air2000, Astraeus, Thomas Cook, Excel Airways, Britannia Airways.

Description:	Los Delfines is located on the west coast of Menorca and is one of the island's three most developed and popular resorts, aimed at package holiday tourists.

The area consists of 3 smaller resorts: Cala'n Forcat, Cala'n Brut and Cala'n Blanes. There are 3 busy beaches, a large choice of restaurants, bars, shops and supermarkets. The main street (Avda. Los Delfines) runs from one end of the resort to the other, remaining close to the beaches all the way.

Although it is a busy resort it is still relatively quiet compared to other Balearic Islands. Likely tenants will be families looking for a well rounded, activity packed holiday. The great thing about this island is that it's cheap to get to. This has kept a steady flow of tenants coming into the area all requiring a property for the week or fortnight. With this increased demand it has led to rental prices shooting up. As a result good yields are being achieved and will be achievable in the foreseeable future.

Hot website:	http://www.menorca-net.co.uk/

Estate Agents:	Name	Address	Tel	Web
	Interealty Balearics	Plaza Santa Ponsa, 4 Local 1 en E-07180, Santa Ponsa, Mallorca	0034 971 699 545/Fax: 0034 971 699 556	www.interealty-mallorca.com.

▶

Estate Agents:	Name	Address	Tel	Web
	H & G C Villas & Apartments	Sue Harvey-Jones Barnhouse Lodge Barnhouse Lane Pulborough RH20 2BS	01798 872 682	www.menorcan villas.info
	Vil-la Inmobiliari	Plaza del Carmen 3 07701 Mahon Menorca Baleares	0034 971 367 852/Fax: 0034 971 368 566	email: Vil-la@vil-la.com
	The Prestige Property Group	No Address	01935 817 188 Fax: 01935 817 199	http://www. prestigeproperty. co.uk email: sales@ prestigeproperty. co.uk
Letting Agents:	**Name**	**Address**	**Tel**	**Web**
	H & G C Villas & Apartments	Sue Harvey-Jones Barnhouse Lodge Barnhouse Lane Pulborough RH20 2BS	01798 872 682	www.menorcan villas.info
	GW Villa Rentals Limited	122 Kimbolton Road, Bedford, Bedfordshire MK41 9DN	01234 344 161	http://www.gw villarentals.com/ email: gillian@ gwvillarentals. com
	Vil-la Inmobiliari	Plaza del Carmen 3 07701 Mahon Menorca Baleares	0034 971 367 852/Fax: 0034 971 368 566	email: Vil-la@vil-la.com

Los Gigantes, Tenerife

Investor profile:	Retirement, Worker, Holiday, Business
Category:	C

Population:	Total	British
	2,400	300

Climate:	Hours of sunshine per day in summer	Days of rain per year	Average spring air temp.	Average summer air temp.	Average autumn air temp.	Average winter air temp.	Average water temp.
	11	33	21.5	27	24	20	21

Proximity to:	Airport	Beach	Nearest city
	35 miles (Reina Sofia)	0.25 miles	60 miles (Santa Cruz)

Educational facilities:	Number of universities	Number of international schools	Number of private schools
	0	0	0

Health services:	Number of public hospitals	Number of private hospitals	Number of private clinics
	0	0	1

Shopping:	Number of shopping centres	Number of markets
	0	0

Restaurants and bars:	Mostly British food and fast food.
Sports and leisure facilities:	Fishing port and marina. Scuba-diving courses. Playa de la Arena beach. Tennis clubs. Hiking tours.

Transport:	Public transport	Roads
	Frequent bus services (run by TITSA) across island's main roads.	Motorways from Santa Cruz.

Crime rate:	Low
Main types of employment:	Mainly tourist and service sectors.
Future plans:	None.
Yield range:	4.9%–5.7%

Type of property:	Entry price	Rent – school holiday peak	Rent – peak	Rent – off peak	Average annual yield
2 bed apartment	180,000	452	362	217	5.7%
3 bed apartment	225,000	542	434	260	5.5%
3 bed townhouse	337,500	723	579	347	4.9%
Villa	396,000	949	759	456	5.5%

Demand for letting:	School holiday peak High	Peak High	Off peak Medium
Finance and leisure scores:	Financial (out of 5) 3	Leisure (out of 5) 3	Total (out of 10) 6
Flights scheduled from:	Gatwick, Heathrow, London City, Luton, Stansted, Bristol, Cardiff, Exeter, Newquay, Plymouth, Bournemouth, Southampton, Birmingham, East Midlands, Humberside, Newcastle, Teesside, Blackpool, Isle of Man, Liverpool, Manchester, Aberdeen, Edinburgh, Glasgow, Inverness, Prestwick, Belfast City, Belfast International, Dublin, Guernsey, Jersey, Norwich, Leeds/Bradford.		
Typical cost of flights:	School holiday peak £154 464	Peak £114–344	Off peak £86–258
Operators:	Monarch, Iberia, Air Europa, BA, BMI, Flyjet, Air2000, Thomas Cook, Astraeus, Britannia Airways, LTE International, My Travel, Excel Airways, Futura.		
Description:	This resort is located on the west coast, set within a rugged coastline consisting of steep cliffs. Considered to be clean, tranquil and very picturesque. However, may be unsuitable for some older people as land is often steep and uneven. Inland is lush compared to the south. It's a popular place with foreign homebuyers which has pushed the property prices beyond some people's reach. Owners have seen their investment rise steeply over the past 3 years and I reckon it will continue even though the prices are high. Yields are not the most exciting but if you can break even then you have done well. You are more than compensated by the growth prospects and the fact that you have a superior holiday home compared to other areas of the island.		
Hot website:	http://www.eurosol.com/		

Estate Agents:	Name	Address	Telt	Web
	Freedom 4 Sale Spain	Antigua Sala de Proyeccion, Antigua Cine de Teguise, Calle Notes 15, Teguise 35530, Lanzarote	0034 928 845 944/Fax: 0034 928 845 936	http://www. freedom4sale. com/
	The Horizon Property Group S.L.	Not disclosed	0161 476 0666 01384 866000	http://www. horizonproperty group.com/
	Eurosol	First Link CC Teide, Local 5 San Eugenio Alto Adeje 38660 Tenerife	0034 922 715 661/Fax: 0034 922 715 953	http://www. eurosol.com/

▶

Letting Agents:	Name	Address	Tel	Web
	Eurosol	First Link CC Teide – Local 5 San Eugenio Alto Adeje 38660 Tenerife	0034 922 715 661/Fax: 0034 922 715 953	http://www. eurosol.com/
	Astliz Estate Agents	P.O. Box 135 Los Gigantes 38683 Santiago del Teide S/C de Tenerife Canary Islands	0034 922 796 776/Fax: 0034 922 796 973	http://www. canaryislands-internet.com/ email: info@ canarian-villas. com

Magaluf, Majorca						
Investor profile:	Retirement, Worker, Holiday, Business					
Category:	A					
Population:	Total 4,800				British 500	
Climate:	Hours of sunshine per day in summer	Days of rain per year	Average spring air temp.	Average summer air temp.	Average autumn air temp.	Average winter air temp.	Average water temp.
	11	65	19	24	21	15	17
Proximity to:	Airport 11 miles (Palma)		Beach 0.25 miles		Nearest city 11 miles (Palma)	
Educational facilities:	Number of universities		Number of international schools		Number of private schools	
	0		0		1	
Health services:	Number of public hospitals		Number of private hospitals		Number of private clinics	
	0		0		1	
Shopping:	Number of shopping centres			Number of markets		
	0			0		
Restaurants and bars:	Predominantly fast food restaurants.					
Sports and leisure facilities:	Watersports. Marineland theme park with dolphin shows, Wild West theme park, Pirate adventure centre. Western Park and Aquacity water-parks open during Summer. Attraction Catamaran – 3-hour boat journey. Choice of nightclubs.					
Transport:	Public transport Restricted.			Roads C-713 from Palma, then exit at Palmanova or along 719 to Palmanova roundabout.		
Crime rate:	High					
Main types of employment:	Mostly service sector.					
Future plans:	Restricted.					
Yield range:	14.7%–17.2%					

▶

Type of property:	Entry price	Rent – school holiday peak	Rent – peak	Rent – off peak	Average annual yield
2 bed apartment	150,250	1,136	909	545	17.2%
3 bed apartment	187,813	1,363	1,091	654	16.5%
3 bed townhouse	281,719	1,818	1,454	872	14.7%
Villa	330,550	2,386	1,908	1,145	16.5%

Demand for letting:	School holiday peak High	Peak High	Off peak Medium

Finance and leisure scores:	Financial (out of 5) 4	Leisure (out of 5) 5	Total (out of 10) 9

Flights scheduled from:	Gatwick, Luton, Stansted, Norwich, Southampton, Bournemouth, Exeter, Bristol, Cardiff, Birmingham, East Midlands, Manchester, Liverpool, Leeds/Bradford, Humberside, Teesside, Newcastle, Glasgow, Glasgow Prestwick, Edinburgh and Aberdeen.

Typical cost of flights:	School holiday peak £115–470	Peak £85–348	Off peak £64–261

Operators:	Air Europa, BMI, Iberia, BA, Air-Berlin, Easyjet, My Travel, Futura, Thomas Cook, Excel Airways, Britannia Airways, Monarch, Air Europa, Air2000, Flyjet.

Description:	Situated on the eastern side of the bay of Palma, Magaluf is a well-developed tourist resort with many high-rise hotels and apartments. It is especially popular with the 18–30 age group.

It is a lively city and a noisy one! Crime rates are high but it's not serious crime, just petty theft, so be sure to go for a site with CCTV or 24-hour security guards.

Rental rates are high due to the demand for accommodation in this area. Your likely tenants are going to be groups of young people but they do pay handsomely. This far outweighs the risk of taking these type of tenants on as any potential damage will be deducted from their sizeable deposit handed over at the point of booking your property.

These yields will not last forever! Property prices will rise so get in early. Magaluf is here to stay so acquiring a property here, in the long term, is of relatively low financial risk. You can easily get flights to this area so it will always appeal to the package holidaymaker.

Hot website:	http://www.mallorcaweb.com/eng/index.html

Estate Agents:	Name	Address	Tel	Web
	The Sun of Majorca	Calle Andratx 32, local 4, 07015 Portals Nous, Mallorca	0034 971 706 570/Fax: 0034 971 706 565	Not disclosed

Estate Agents:	Name	Address	Tel	Web
	Interealty Balearics	Plaza Santa Ponsa, 4 Local 1 en E-07180, Santa Ponsa, Mallorca	0034 971 699 545/Fax: 0034 971 699 556	www.interealty-mallorca.com
	Roberto Jaime Gourlay	Apartado 1423, Palma De Mallorca	0034 971 681 873/Fax: 0034 971 680 320	http://www.mallorca-real-estate.com email: robertog @ocea.es.com/
	Sea Green	Cala Bona Palma de Mallorca	Not known	http://www.mallorca-penthouse.de email: peter@ kerler.de
Letting Agents:	Name	Address	Tel	Web
	Interealty Balearics	Plaza Santa Ponsa, 4 Local 1 en E-07180, Santa Ponsa, Mallorca	0034 971 699 545/Fax: 0034 971 699 556	www.interealty-mallorca.com
	Europa Inmobiliaria	Antoni Maria Alcover nº 47 Palma	0034 971 676 787/Fax: 0034 971 676 567	http://www.europa-inmobiliaria.com email: europa @europa-inmobiliaria.com
	Arko Inmobiliario	Avda. Son Rapinya, nº 8 1º C, Palma de Mallorca	0034 619 226 688/971 453 689/Fax: 0034 971 457 900	email: arco inmobiliario@ hotmail.com

Mahon, Menorca		
Investor profile:	Retirement, Worker, Holiday, Business	
Category:	A	
Population:	Total 25,000	British 1,500

Climate:	Hours of sunshine per day in summer	Days of rain per year	Average spring air temp.	Average summer air temp.	Average autumn air temp.	Average winter air temp.	Average water temp.
	11	65	20	27	23	13	17

Proximity to:	Airport 3 miles (Mahon)	Beach 0.25–2 miles	Nearest city Mahon
Educational facilities:	Number of universities 0	Number of international schools 1	Number of private schools 2
Health services:	Number of public hospitals 1	Number of private hospitals 0	Number of private clinics 6

Shopping:	Number of shopping centres 1	Number of markets 1

Restaurants and bars:	Most bars found in Anden Poniente are near port. The number of restaurants and bars is smaller than on other Balearic Islands, and many restaurants close in off-peak season. Variety of international cuisine available.
Sports and leisure facilities:	Horse-riding stables. Speedboats at port. Aero-club with go-kart track, snooker, pool and table tennis tables and a bridge club. Aquarium (at port). Glass bottom boat rides from port. Classical music concerts throughout the year. Organ recitals at Mahon cathedral. Theatre productions at the Teatro Principal. Menorca Cricket Club and International Rotary Club for expatriates. Military museum.

Transport:	Public transport Regular bus service between Mahon and Ciutadella.	Roads One main road through centre of island between Mahon and Ciutadella.

Crime rate:	Low
Main types of employment:	Tourist sector during peak season. Limited number of foreign workers.
Future plans:	Increased size of national parks and marine reserves.
Yield range:	21.9%–25.7%

Type of property:	Entry price	Rent – school holiday peak	Rent – peak	Rent – off peak	Average annual yield
2 bed apartment	133,000	1,500	1,200	720	25.7%
3 bed apartment	166,250	1,800	1,440	864	24.7%
3 bed townhouse	249,375	2,400	1,920	1,152	21.9%
Villa	292,600	3,150	2,520	1,512	24.5%

Demand for letting:	School holiday peak High		Peak High		Off peak Low

Finance and leisure scores:	Financial (out of 5) 5	Leisure (out of 5) 4	Total (out of 10) 9

Flights scheduled from:	Gatwick, Luton, Stansted, Bournemouth, Bristol, Cardiff, Birmingham, East Midlands, Manchester, Liverpool, Leeds/Bradford, Humberside, Teesside, Newcastle, Glasgow, Edinburgh.

Typical cost of flights:	School holiday peak £120–543	Peak £89–402	Off peak £67–302

Operators:	Monarch, Iberia, BA, My Travel, Air2000, Astraeus, Thomas Cook, Excel Airways, Britannia Airways.

Description:	Mahon is the capital of Menorca – the second largest island in the Balearics. The city is situated on the east coast of the island and has its own port and harbour.

Property consists of mainly low-level buildings of Moorish and British architecture. There are several historical buildings, including the Arch de San Roque, the Town Hall, (built in 1631) and the Church of Santa Maria (rebuilt between 1748 and 1772).

There are relatively few high-rise buildings and the city is more tranquil compared to other Balearic islands. The British are the main foreign purchasers of property in the area, and Menorca has the cheapest property out of all the Balearic Islands.

Although it is a busy resort it is still relatively quiet compared to other Balearic Islands. Likely tenants will be families looking for a well rounded, activity packed holiday. The great thing about this island is that it's cheap to get to. This has kept a steady flow of tenants coming into the area all requiring a property for the week or fortnight. With this increased demand it has led to rental prices shooting up. As a result fantastic yields are being achieved and good yields, at the very least, will be achievable in the foreseeable future.

Hot website:	http://www.menorca-net.co.uk/

Estate Agents:	Name	Address	Tel	Web
	The Prestige Property Group	No Address	01935 817188 Fax: 01935 817199	http://www. prestige property.co.uk email: sales@ prestigeproperty. co.uk

Estate Agents:	Name	Address	Tel	Web
	Interealty Balearics	Plaza Santa Ponsa, 4 Local 1 en E-07180, Santa Ponsa, Mallorca	0034 971 699 545/Fax: 0034 971 699 556	www.interealty-mallorca.com
	H & G C Villas & Apartments	Sue Harvey-Jones Barnhouse Lodge Barnhouse Lane Pulborough RH20 2BS	01798 872 682	www.menorcan villas.info
	Vil-la Inmobiliari	Plaza del Carmen 3 07701 Mahon Menorca	0034 971 367 852/Fax: 0034 971 368 566	email: Vil-la@vil-la.com
Letting Agents:	**Name**	**Address**	**Tel**	**Web**
	GW Villa Rentals Limited	122 Kimbolton Road, Bedford, Bedfordshire MK41 9DN	01234 344 161	http://www.gw villarentals.com/ email: gillian@ gwvillarentals. com
	Vil-la Inmobiliari	Plaza del Carmen 3 07701 Mahon Menorca	0034 971 367 852/Fax: 0034 971 368 566	email: Vil-la@vil-la.com
	H & G C Villas & Apartments	Sue Harvey-Jones Barnhouse Lodge Barnhouse Lane Pulborough RH20 2BS	01798 872 682	www.menorcan villas.info

Malaga, Costa del Sol

Investor profile:	Retirement, Worker, Holiday, Business
Category:	C

Population:	Total	British
	540,000	6,000

Climate:	Hours of sunshine per day in summer	Days of rain per year	Average spring air temp.	Average summer air temp.	Average autumn air temp.	Average winter air temp.	Average water temp.
	11	45	21	28	24	16	20

Proximity to:	Airport	Beach	Nearest city
	4 miles (Malaga)	0.5 miles	Malaga

Educational facilities:	Number of universities	Number of international schools	Number of private schools
	1	3	9

Health services:	Number of public hospitals	Number of private hospitals	Number of private clinics
	5	0	2

Shopping:	Number of shopping centres	Number of markets
	5	2

Restaurants and bars:	Most restaurants offer Spanish cuisine. In the east of the city fried fish, the local speciality, is widely available. Many tapas bars in the old town.
Sports and leisure facilities:	Jose Maria Martin Carpena sports pavilion in west end. Rosaleda football stadium in the north of the city. 2 sailing clubs. 2 golf courses on city outskirts. Summer fair at beginning of August. Annual cinema and jazz festivals. Opera, jazz and classical concerts at Cervantes Theatre in old town throughout the year. Alameda Park botanical garden. 2 further botanical gardens on city outskirts. Choice of multi-screen cinemas and smaller cinemas.

Transport:	Public transport	Roads
	40 bus routes across the city. RENFE train services from Esplanada de la Estacion.	N-340 from Almeria, Cadiz and Estepona. A-92 and N-331 from Granada and Seville.

Crime rate:	High
Main types of employment:	Varied, but particularly in technological industry.
Future plans:	Large congress centre. New museum, shopping centre, auditorium and leisure complex near port. New road developments – new ring road around north and west of city and new access to airport.
Yield range:	3.8%–4.5%

Type of property:	Entry price	Rent – school holiday peak	Rent – peak	Rent – off peak	Average annual yield
2 bed apartment	91,122	178	142	85	4.5%
3 bed apartment	113,903	214	171	103	4.3%
3 bed townhouse	170,854	285	228	137	3.8%
Villa	200,468	374	299	179	4.3%

Demand for letting:	School holiday peak High		Peak High		Off peak High

Finance and leisure scores:	Financial (out of 5) 2		Leisure (out of 5) 4		Total (out of 10) 6

Flights scheduled from:	Gatwick, Heathrow, London City, Luton, Stansted, Bristol, Cardiff, Exeter, Newquay, Plymouth, Bournemouth, Southampton, Birmingham, East Midlands, Humberside, Newcastle, Teesside, Blackpool, Isle of Man, Liverpool, Manchester, Aberdeen, Edinburgh, Glasgow, Inverness, Belfast City, Belfast International, Derry, Cork, Dublin, Guernsey, Jersey, Norwich, Leeds/Bradford.

Typical cost of flights:	School holiday peak £201–320		Peak £149–237		Off peak £112–178

Operators:	Monarch, Swiss International, BA, Air France, Excel Airways, Futura, Thomas Cook, Astraeus, Air 2000, My Travel, Easyjet.

Description:	Malaga is the fifth largest city in Spain. A Moorish history is evident, in particular the Alcazaba fortress and the Gibralfaro castle. The old town has narrow streets surrounding the cathedral and can prove to be an interesting walk. The modern part of town has the bus and railway station and is west of Guadalmedina river.
	It has a busy port which keeps employment levels high and therefore tenant demand high throughout the year. It has a less crowded beach than other parts of the coast as most holidaymakers choose the more built-up resorts. The majority of residents are Spanish but the British population has increased at a greater rate than most other areas.
	The university and science park in the Teatinos district is in the west of the city and there are several exclusive residential areas – Colonia de Santa Ines and Puerto de la Torre behind the Teatinos district – which have been quite popular with the British. Cerrado de Calderon, Limonar, Malagueta and Pedregalejo are east of the city centre and have also been quite popular.
	The property market in Malaga is a stable one due to longer-term residences compared with other coastal resorts. The market is made up of mostly apartments – houses tend to be limited too exclusive areas. Property is cheaper than other parts of coast, except for the exclusive areas – it's just a matter of time before these cheaper properties catch up so there is plenty of scope for capital growth. Prices have gradually risen in the past few years and demand is high for most of the year due to a large university population.
Hot website:	http://www.malagaturismo.com/menus/eng/marco.htm

Estate Agents:	Name	Address	Tel	Web
	Andalucia Real Estate	No address	0034 653 619 696/Fax: 0034 952 174 443	http://www. andaluciareal estate.com/
	Alcoba Cabello	Avda. Vibar Tellez 39, 29770 Velez Malaga	0034 952 502 445/Fax: 0034 952 501 262	Not disclosed
	Universal Real Estate	Avda. Palma de Mallorca, 27	Not disclosed	info@inmo-universal.com
	El Congreso Real Estate	Pedro Campos Ed. Congreso, 1 A	0034 952 384 183	Not disclosed
Letting Agents:	Name	Address	Tel	Web
	Country Properties S.A.	Plaza Almijara, Competa Malaga	0034 952 516 178	website: http:// www.country properties.net email: sales@ country properties.net
	Mab Costa del Sol	Apdo. 121 Malaga	0034 666 066 050	email: ysl@ole. com
	Costa del Sol Online Properties	Avda. de la Constitucion 37, Edificio Gavilan nº 9 Malaga	0034 952 563 021/Fax: 0034 952 575 464	website: http:// www.finda homeinspain email: info@ findahome inspain.com
	Villas Sayalonga S.L.	C/Calvario s/n Sayalonga Malaga	0034 952 535 043	email: info@ villasaya.com

Marbella, Costa del Sol

Investor profile:	Retirement, Worker, Holiday, Business		
Category:	A		

Population:	Total 110,000	British 14,000

Climate:	Hours of sunshine per day in summer	Days of rain per year	Average spring air temp.	Average summer air temp.	Average autumn air temp.	Average winter air temp.	Average water temp.
	11	45	21	28	24	16	20

Proximity to:	Airport 29 miles (Malaga)	Beach 0.25 miles	Nearest city 32 miles (Malaga)

Educational facilities:	Number of universities	Number of international schools	Number of private schools
	0	8	19

Health services:	Number of public hospitals	Number of private hospitals	Number of private clinics
	1	2	16

Shopping:	Number of shopping centres	Number of markets
	10	2

Restaurants and bars:	Huge variety including Lebanese, Moroccan, French, Japanese, Greek, Russian and Thai. Also beach restaurants and tea rooms.
Sports and leisure facilities:	Several public sports centres and many private sport centres including tennis clubs and a sailing club in the port. Variety of sports available including diving, horse-riding, golf, hunting, skiing (Sierra Nevada) and nautical sports. 10 golf courses in area. 6 nightclubs in Marbella itself, 1 in Nueva Andalucia and 7 in Puerto Banus. Cinemas, theatres, exhibition halls and museums. Also theme parks, water parks and bull fighting rings.

Transport:	**Public transport** Bus services every 45 minutes (Mon-Fri) to Malaga. Also services to Madrid, Granada, Seville, Almeria and rest of Costa del Sol including Malaga airport.	**Roads** A-7 bypass to the north. N-340 around the city centre.

Crime rate:	Low
Main types of employment:	Mainly tourist and service sectors, particularly in the property market.
Future plans:	Restricted.
Yield range:	8.6%–10.0%

▶

Type of property:	Entry price	Rent – school holiday peak	Rent – peak	Rent – off peak	Average annual yield
2 bed apartment	204,000	899	719	432	10.0%
3 bed apartment	255,000	1,079	863	518	9.6%
3 bed townhouse	382,500	1,438	1,151	690	8.6%
Villa	448,800	1,888	1,510	906	9.6%

Demand for letting:	School holiday peak High	Peak Medium	Off peak Medium

Finance and leisure scores:	Financial (out of 5) 4	Leisure (out of 5) 5	Total (out of 10) 9

Flights scheduled from:	Gatwick, Heathrow, London City, Luton, Stansted, Bristol, Cardiff, Exeter, Newquay, Plymouth, Bournemouth, Southampton, Birmingham, East Midlands, Humberside, Newcastle, Teesside, Blackpool, Isle of Man, Liverpool, Manchester, Aberdeen, Edinburgh, Glasgow, Inverness, Belfast City, Belfast International, Derry, Cork, Dublin, Guernsey, Jersey, Norwich, Leeds/Bradford.

Typical cost of flights:	School holiday peak £201–320	Peak £149–237	Off peak £112–178

Operators:	Monarch, Swiss International, BA, Air France, Excel Airways, Futura, Thomas Cook, Astraeus, Air 2000, My Travel, Easyjet.

Description:	Marbella is located beneath the Sierra Blanca mountain range and is divided into two main parts – the old town, surrounded by Moorish fortress walls and characterised by narrow streets, and the new town, characterised by wide tree-lined avenues and high-rise blocks. Exclusive developments such as Hacienda Las Chapas, Los Monteros, El Rosario, Nagueles ('Golden Mile') and Nueva Andalucia surround the town and are made up of mostly luxurious mansions.
	I would consider this to be the best part of Costa del Sol. To the west of Marbella lies the famous leisure marina, Puerto Banus, where anyone who's anyone can be found. The beach stretch of Marbella is massive, totalling 26 km, so you'll have no trouble finding a suitable sun bathing spot. In the centre of the old town there is the Orange Square where there are stately buildings, small shops, art galleries, bars and bistros to keep you busy.
	Even though the property prices are high so are the rents. Yields are around 9% which is quite respectable compared to what you can get in the UK. You will never be short of a tenant as long as your property is up to scratch. People of this area expect a lot and if they get it they'll pay well for it!

Hot website:	http://www.marbella.com/eng/

Estate Agents:	Name	Address	Tel	Web
	Agencia Inmobiliaria Panorama	Boulevard Principe Alfonso de Hohenlohe 29600 Marbella	0034 902 111 114/Fax: 0034 952 822 111	http://www. panorama.es/ email: info@ @panorama.es
	Anna and Ivar Dahl, Real Estate	Urb. Marbellamar, Loc.1-C 29600 Marbella	0034 952 765 045/Fax: 0034 952 776 816	http://www.i vardahl.com/ email: real estate@ivardahl. com
	James Molina, S.L.	Arturo Rubinstein 29600 Marbella	0034 952 868 858/Fax: 0034 952 868 314	http://www.j jamesmolina. com/ email: james molina@ wanadoo.es
	Tessa Group	C/ Jacinto Benavente, 37 29600 Marbella	0034 952 868 827/ Mob: 0034 699 060 646	http://www. pgb.es/tessa group/iventas. html email: tessagroup @terra.es
Letting Agents:	Name	Address	Tel	Web
	Agencia Inmobiliaria Panorama	Boulevard Principe Alfonso de Hohenlohe 29600 Marbella	0034 902 111 114/Fax: 0034 952 822 111	http://www. panorama.es/ email: info@ panorama.es
	Viva Estates	C.C. Reserva del Alvarito Urb. Andasol – CN-340, Km 189 29600 Marbella	0034 952 831 100/Fax: 0034 952 831 107	http://www. vivaestates.com/ email: viva@ vivaestates.com
	Sarena, S.A.	Urb. La Mairena (Altos de Elviria) 29600 Marbella	0034 952 836 092/Fax: 0034 952 839 378	http://www. mairena.com/ email: mairena @mairena.com
	Sitio de Calahonda Properties	Oficina de Ventas, C.N. 340 Km 196 Mijas Costa 29650 Marbella	0034 952 933 140/Fax: 0034 952 934 342	http://www. sitiodecala honda.com/ email: info@ sitiodecala honda.com

Miami Playa, Costa Dorada

Investor profile:	Retirement, Worker, Holiday, Business
Category:	C

Population:	Total 3,760	British 300

Climate:	Hours of sunshine per day in summer	Days of rain per year	Average spring air temp.	Average summer air temp.	Average autumn air temp.	Average winter air temp.	Average water temp.
	9	102	17	27	24	12	19

Proximity to:	Airport 20 miles (Reus)	Beach 0.25 miles	Nearest city 22 miles (Tarragona)

Educational facilities:	Number of universities	Number of international schools	Number of private schools
	0	0	0

Health services:	Number of public hospitals	Number of private hospitals	Number of private clinics
	0	0	0

Shopping:	Number of shopping centres	Number of markets
	0	0

Restaurants and bars:	Predominantly international cuisine. Also many English pubs.
Sports and leisure facilities:	18-hole golf course and watersport facilities in the area. Horse-riding stables. Tennis clubs. Most leisure facilities within hotel and apartment complexes.

Transport:	Public transport	Roads
	Train services from Barcelona and Valencia. Local and regional bus services.	A-7 motorway from Calafell to southern Costa Dorada. A-16 from Castelldefels (near Barcelona) to Calafell. N-340 single carriageway motorway along coast.

Crime rate:	Low.
Main types of employment:	Mainly tourist sector.
Future plans:	New residential developments in area.
Yield range:	9.5%–11.1%

Type of property:	Entry price	Rent – school holiday peak	Rent – peak	Rent – off peak	Average annual yield
2 bed apartment	144,500	705	564	338	11.1%
3 bed apartment	180,625	846	677	406	10.7%
3 bed townhouse	270,938	1,128	902	541	9.5%
Villa	317,900	1,481	1,184	711	10.6%

Demand for letting:	School holiday peak Medium	Peak Medium	Off peak Low

Finance and leisure scores:	Financial (out of 5) 4	Leisure (out of 5) 2	Total (out of 10) 6

Flights scheduled from:	Gatwick, Heathrow, Luton, Stansted, Bristol, Cardiff, Birmingham, East Midlands, Newcastle, Teesside, Liverpool, Manchester, Leeds/Bradford, Glasgow, Inverness, Belfast International, Dublin.

Typical cost of flights:	School holiday peak £116–235	Peak £86–174	Off peak £65–131

Operators:	Monarch, Air 2000, Thomas Cook, Britannia Airways, BA, Excel Airways, My Travel.

Description:	Miami Playa is a seaside resort located 20 minutes south of Salou (see p.130). There are no high-rise blocks or apartments, the beaches are far less crowded, and nightlife is limited. The resort has broad streets, with its residential areas a good distance form the main tourist resorts. The beaches are set in sand and shingle bays, overlooked by rocky cliffs. Within the resort there are many developments consisting of villas, chalets and low-rise flats. Miami Playa is popular with foreign homebuyers such as the British, German, French, Dutch and Swiss, as well as the Spanish and local Catalans. It's very cheap to get here even in the peak season. If you book on the internet you could get a return flight for less than £50! This area makes a great holiday home for the family and can provide a nice income to cover all costs of the property. It's a 'non-resort' resort area and gives you an alternative to what we know as a Spanish holiday. If I had to go for one area that offered the best capital growth then this would be it – do I need to say anymore!

Hot website:	http://www.costadaurada.org/costadaurada-oa/pagines/uk/index.html

Estate Agents:	Name	Address	Tel	Web
	Asesoramiento y Venta Immobiiaria	Avda. Barcelona 92–98, Local 7 Miami Playa	0034 977 170 474/Fax: 0034 977 170 474	http://www.handelshaus-miami.com email: j.stoeber@handelshaus-miami.com

Estate Agents:	Name	Address	Tel	Web
	Costa Dorada Real Estate	Mont Roig del Camp Costa Dorada	0034 977 179 661/Fax: 0034 977 170 876	http://www. costa-dorada-casa-finca.com/ email: info@ dorfmann.com
	Lacey and Co	65 Priory Avenue, Southend-on-Sea, Essex SS2 69A	01702 603 210 Fax: 01702 603 211	Not disclosed
Letting Agents:	**Name**	**Address**	**Tel**	**Web**
	Universal Holiday Centre	C/ Bruselas, 39 Salou Tarragona	0034 977 353 010/Fax: 0034 977 353 448	http://www. universalholiday centre.com/ indexb.html email: info@ universalholiday centre.com

Mijas, Costa del Sol

Investor profile:	Retirement, Worker, Holiday, Business		
Category:	A		
Population:	Total 45,000		British 6,000

Climate:	Hours of sunshine per day in summer	Days of rain per year	Average spring air temp.	Average summer air temp.	Average autumn air temp.	Average winter air temp.	Average water temp.
	11	45	21	28	24	16	20

Proximity to:	Airport 16.5 miles (Malaga)	Beach 0.25 miles	Nearest city 19 miles (Malaga)
Educational facilities:	Number of universities 0	Number of international schools 1	Number of private schools 2
Health services:	Number of public hospitals 0	Number of private hospitals 0	Number of private clinics 7

Shopping:	Number of shopping centres 1	Number of markets 3

Restaurants and bars:	Narrower choice of restaurants and bars relative to other areas on Costa del Sol, but local, international and British food all available.
Sports and leisure facilities:	Mijas Village football field and polysport pavilion. Public Gymnasium. La Cala Golf Resort north of Mijas village (2 18-hole courses). La Siesta Golf (9-hole course). Mijas Golf (2 18-hole courses). Miraflores 18-hole golf course. Valle del Golf Resort. 2 go-karting clubs. Horse race course and riding school. Mijas aquatic park on the Fuengirola bypass with water slides and wave pools (open between May and September). Historical, Miniature and Bullfighting museums. Mijas fair in September and annual theatre festival in Summer. English-language films screened at cinema in Mijas Costa.

Transport:	**Public transport** Regular bus service to Fuengirola (every half hour on weekdays).	**Roads** Autovia del Sol from Malaga. MA-409 from Fuengirola. N-340 and MA-409 from Marbella. MA-485 from Benalmadena.
Crime rate:	Low	
Main types of employment:	Tourist and service sectors, especially property market.	
Future plans:	None	

Yield range:	12.9%–15.2%				
Type of property:	Entry price	Rent – school holiday peak	Rent – peak	Rent – off peak	Average annual yield
2 bed apartment	120,000	798	638	383	15.2%
3 bed apartment	150,000	958	766	460	14.6%
3 bed townhouse	225,000	1,277	1,021	613	12.9%
Villa	264,000	1,676	1,341	804	14.5%
Demand for letting:	School holiday peak High		Peak High		Off peak Medium
Finance and leisure scores:	Financial (out of 5) 5		Leisure (out of 5) 5		Total (out of 10) 10
Flights scheduled from:	Gatwick, Heathrow, London City, Luton, Stansted, Bristol, Cardiff, Exeter, Newquay, Plymouth, Bournemouth, Southampton, Birmingham, East Midlands, Humberside, Newcastle, Teesside, Blackpool, Isle of Man, Liverpool, Manchester, Aberdeen, Edinburgh, Glasgow, Inverness, Belfast City, Belfast International, Derry, Cork, Dublin, Guernsey, Jersey, Norwich, Leeds/Bradford.				
Typical cost of flights:	School holiday peak £201–320		Peak £149–237		Off peak £112–178
Operators:	Monarch, Swiss International, BA, Air France, Excel Airways, Futura, Thomas Cook, Astraeus, Air 2000, My Travel, Easyjet.				
Description:	Mijas consists of a small Andalusian village located in the mountains above Fuengirola, and also of the area between Fuengirola and port Cabopino, known as Mijas Costa. Mijas Costa is made up of several residential developments such as Calahonda, El Chaparral, El Faro, La Cala, Miraflores, Riviera del Sol and Torrevieja. These residential complexes are home to many of the area's ex-patriot population, composed mainly of British, Germans and Scandinavians. Calahonda and Riviera del Sol are mainly inhabited by a British population. Mijas village has very narrow and steep streets (limited to pedestrians and donkeys) and has Roman, Moorish and Spanish monuments. Property in the village is more expensive than outside of it. Stick to the complexes. I struggle to find what's wrong with this place. If I was pushed I would say that demand tails off for some of the off peak season. Otherwise the yields are great, the properties are of good value, there's loads to do, it has low crime rates and it's easy to get to – what more do you want!				
Hot website:	http://mijas-spain.travel-holiday-guide.co.uk/				

Estate Agents:	Name	Address	Tel	Web
	Sol Agency Ltd	Not disclosed	Spanish Office Telephone/Fax: 0034 952 668 708 UK Freephone for Property Sales enquiries: 0800 198 2927	http://www.sol-agency.com/index.htm email: info@ sol-agency.com
	The Costa del Sol Property Index S.L.	Jarales de Alhamar, Calahonda, Mijas Costa, Malaga, España	Tel 0034 952 931 603/Fax: 0034 952 931 847	http://www. property-spain.com/costa delsolproperty index.htm email: sales@ property-spain. com
	Coastal Realty S.L.	Conjunto Casaño Oficina B4 Avda. Manolete Nueva Andalucia Marbella 29660	0034 952 816 088/Fax: 0034 952 814 062 Mob: 0034 699 434 384	http://www. coastal-realty. co.uk/houses_ for_sale_mijas_ spain.html email: info@ bargain-properties.com
	Andersen & Andersen Estates S.L.	Centro Idea, Ctra. De Mijas Km 3,6, 29650 Mijas, Malaga	0034 952 462 450/Fax: 0034 952 462 184	http://www.aa estates.com/ email: info@aa estates.com
Letting Agents:	Name	Address	Tel	Web
	Sol Agency Ltd	Not disclosed	Spanish Office Telephone/Fax: 0034 952 668 708 UK Freephone for Property Sales enquiries: 0800 198 2927	http://www.sol-agency.com/index.htm email: info@ sol-agency.com
	Mijas Villas Ltd	Ian Fishwick Mijas Villas Ltd Heysome House Crank Hill Crank St. Helens WA11 7SF	01744 884404 Fax: 01744 883019 Spain: 0034 654 439 745	http://www. mijas-villas. com/index.htm email: enquiries@ mijas-villas. com

Letting Agents:	Name	Address	Tel	Web
	Riviera Estates	Riviera del Sol El saladito 1 Bajo 6 29649 Mijas Costa (Malaga)	0034 952 932 681 Fax: 0034 952 935 160	http://www. rivieraestate spain.net/ email: miguel@ rivieraestate spain.net
	Mijas Costa Estates S.L.	Mansion Alhamar, Ctr. Cadiz Km.197 Mijas Costa, Malaga	0034 952 931 124 Mob: 0034 647 920 388	Website: http:// www.mijascosta estates.com email: brian@ mijascosta estates.com

Nerja, Costa del Sol

Investor profile:	Retirement, Worker, Holiday, Business						
Category:	C						

Population:	Total 16,000				British 1,800		

Climate:	Hours of sunshine per day in summer	Days of rain per year	Average spring air temp.	Average summer air temp.	Average autumn air temp.	Average winter air temp.	Average water temp.
	11	45	21	28	24	16	20

Proximity to:	Airport 38 miles (Malaga)	Beach 0.25 miles	Nearest city 34 miles (Malaga)

Educational facilities:	Number of universities	Number of international schools	Number of private schools
	0	0	0

Health services:	Number of public hospitals	Number of private hospitals	Number of private clinics
	0	0	1

Shopping:	Number of shopping centres	Number of markets
	0	2

Restaurants and bars:	Wide selection of international restaurants, more expensive in Balcon area. Seafood beach restaurants.

Sports and leisure facilities:	Scubanerja dive centre. Golf course. Music and ballet festival in Nerja caves during Summer. Nightlife concentrated around Plaza Tutti Frutti.

Transport:	**Public transport** Limited bus service. Private transport recommended.	**Roads** N-340 dual carriageway to Nerja from rest of coast. N-323 and N-340 from Granada.

Crime rate:	Low

Main types of employment:	Mostly in service sector, during Summer.

Future plans:	Train service from Malaga to Nerja.

Yield range:	5.7%–6.7%

Type of property:	Entry price	Rent – school holiday peak	Rent – peak	Rent – off peak	Average annual yield
2 bed apartment	127,600	376	301	180	6.7%
3 bed apartment	159,500	451	361	217	6.4%
3 bed townhouse	239,250	602	481	289	5.7%
Villa	280,720	790	632	379	6.4%

Demand for letting:	School holiday peak High	Peak High	Off peak Low
Finance and leisure scores:	Financial (out of 5) 2	Leisure (out of 5) 3	Total (out of 10) 5
Flights scheduled from:	Gatwick, Heathrow, London City, Luton, Stansted, Bristol, Cardiff, Exeter, Newquay, Plymouth, Bournemouth, Southampton, Birmingham, East Midlands, Humberside, Newcastle, Teesside, Blackpool, Isle of Man, Liverpool, Manchester, Aberdeen, Edinburgh, Glasgow, Inverness, Belfast City, Belfast International, Derry, Cork, Dublin, Guernsey, Jersey, Norwich, Leeds/Bradford.		
Typical cost of flights:	School holiday peak £201–320	Peak £149–237	Off peak £112–178
Operators:	Monarch, Swiss International, BA, Air France, Excel Airways, Futura, Thomas Cook, Astraeus, Air 2000, My Travel, Easyjet.		
Description:	Nerja is located below the Sierra Almijara mountains, with 5 sandy beaches stretched over 6 miles. 　　This area is a little gem. It has a more traditional Spanish character with not as many high-rise apartment and hotel blocks as other resorts and is less lively. It is instead characterised by an old town, limestone caves and a tree-lined promenade (Balcon de Europa). Monuments in the town include El Salvador church (1505), Ermita de Ntra. Sra. de las Angustias (1720) and Torre de Macaca (1497). 　　Property is slightly more expensive than other parts of eastern Costa del Sol particularly in the village of Frigiliana. It's a popular place with foreign homebuyers which has pushed the property prices beyond some people's reach. Owners have seen their investment rise steeply over the past 5 years and I reckon it will continue even though the prices are high. Yields are not the most exciting but if you can break even then you have done well. You are more than compensated by the growth prospects and the fact that you have a superior holiday home compared to other areas on the coast.		
Hot website:	http://www.nerja.to/		

Estate Agents:	Name	Address	Tel	Web
	Playa Properties S.L.	Calle Pintada, 10 – 29780 Nerja	0034 952 523 399/Fax: 0034 952 523 316	http://www. playaproperties. com/ email: real estate@playa properties.com
	Nerjaproperty shop.com	Avda. Castilla Pérez, 66, bajo 29780 Nerja	0034 952 521 303/Fax: 0034 952 527 162	http://www. nerjaproperty shop.com/site/ en.html email: info@ nerjaproperty shop.com

▶

Estate Agents:	Name	Address	Tel	Web
	Nerja Properties	Jose Martín Avda. Castilla Pérez, 20 29780 Nerja	0034 952 525 462/Fax: 0034 952 526 679	email: info@ nerjaproperties sl.com
	Certuner, S.L. Real Estate	Avda. Mediterraneo, Edif. Toboso II Nerja	0034 952 523 872	http://www. certuner.com/ email: certuner@ teleline.es
Letting Agents:	Name	Address	Tel	Web
	Nerjaproperty shop.com	Avda. Castilla Pérez, 66, bajo 29780 Nerja	0034 952 521 303/Fax: 0034 952 527 162	http://www. nerjaproperty shop.com/site/ en.html email: info@ nerjaproperty shop.com
	Pinto Estate	C/ Antonio Ferrandis Chanquete, nº 9 Nerja	0034 952 528 390/Fax: 0034 952 526 567	website: http:// www.pinto estate.com email: info@ pintoestate.com
	Interealty	Plaza Cavana, 10, 29780 Nerja	0034 952 527 083/Fax 0034 952 527 035	email: info@ interealty.es

Orihuela Costa, Costa Blanca

Investor profile:	Retirement, Worker, Holiday, Business		
Category:	C		
Population:	Total 56,000		British 1,000

Climate:	Hours of sunshine per day in summer	Days of rain per year	Average spring air temp.	Average summer air temp.	Average autumn air temp.	Average winter air temp.	Average water temp.
	11	42	21	30	24	17	18

Proximity to:	Airport 21 miles (Murcia)	Beach 0.25 miles	Nearest city 21 miles (Murcia)

Educational facilities:	Number of universities	Number of international schools	Number of private schools
	0	0	0

Health services:	Number of public hospitals	Number of private hospitals	Number of private clinics
	1	0	2

Shopping:	Number of shopping centres	Number of markets
	0	0

Restaurants and bars:	International and local cuisine available. Fast food on the coast.
Sports and leisure facilities:	Six 18-hole golf courses and five marinas in the area (e.g. Cabo Roig and Dehesa de Campoamor) offering a variety of watersports such as scuba-diving and windsurfing. Classical music and theatre shows. 2 cinemas and 8 museums in town.

Transport:	Public transport Restricted. Private transport recommended.	Roads N-332 from Murcia, Benidorm and Valencia.

Crime rate:	Medium
Main types of employment:	Tourist and service sectors.
Future plans:	Traffic control systems on N-332. New construction of houses/hotels/apartments. Like Torrevieja (see p.145), Orihuela Costa is a fast-developing resort.
Yield range:	9.7%–10.9%

Type of property:	Entry price	Rent – school holiday peak	Rent – peak	Rent – off peak	Average annual yield
2 bed apartment	101,363	453	362	217	10.2%
3 bed apartment	121,636	544	435	261	10.2%
3 bed townhouse	152,045	725	580	348	10.9%
Villa	223,000	951	761	457	9.7%

Demand for letting:	School holiday peak High	Peak High	Off peak Medium

Finance and leisure scores:	Financial (out of 5) 3	Leisure (out of 5) 3	Total (out of 10) 6

Flights scheduled from:	Gatwick, Heathrow, London City, Stansted, Bristol, Newquay, Plymouth, Southampton, Birmingham, East Midlands, Newcastle, Isle of Man, Manchester, Aberdeen, Edinburgh, Glasgow, Inverness, Belfast City, Belfast International, Cork, Dublin, Guernsey, Jersey, Leeds/Bradford.

Typical cost of flights:	School holiday peak £266–803	Peak £197–595	Off peak £148–446

Operators:	Iberia, Air Europa, Astraeus.

Description:	Orihuela Costa is the 10 mile-long coastline located near the inland town of Orihuela, on the southern part of the Costa Blanca. The area consists of beaches with coves and is lined with palm trees. There are also almond and olive groves.
	The town of Orihuela is itself historic. There are 14 historical sites in total, including Catedral del San Salvador y Santa Maria and the Palacio Rubalcava. There are several residential developments in the area, such as Cabo Roig, Dehesa de Campoamor, La Zenia, Playa Flamenca and Punta Prima. These areas have gained popularity with both Spanish and foreign homebuyers.
	There are not many British here but this will all change. Numerous developments are springing up here and the biggest buyers have been the British. The yields achievable here are promising, though not exciting. What I do find exciting however, is the opportunity for capital gain. Once developed the property prices will mirror the prices being achieved in the rest of Costa Blanca.

Hot website:	http://www.costablanca.org/eng/index.asp

Estate Agents:	Name	Address	Tel	Web
	International Sunline Properties S.L.	Centro Comercial Zenia Mar Orihuela-Costa Alicante	0034 966 761 818/Fax: 0034 966 760 164	http://www. sunline.ws email: jonathan @sunline.ws
	Austro Inmo S.L.	Calle Nicolas Debussy 1140 Orihuela Costa	0034 966 730 762/Fax: 0034 966 773 341	http://www. austroinmo.com email: austro-inmo@cesser. com

Estate Agents:	Name	Address	Tel	Web
	Haart	P.O. Box 5995 Colchester Essex CO3 3WR	0845 600 7778	http://www. tmxhaart.co.uk/ email: web master@haart. co.uk
	Freedom 4 Sale Spain	Antigua Sala de Proyeccion, Antigua Cine de Teguise, Calle Notes 15, Teguise 35530, Lanzarote	0034 928 845 944/Fax: 0034 928 845 936	http://www. freedom4sale. com/

Letting Agents:	Name	Address	Tel	Web
	Costa Blanca Rentals	Suite 173, Ctra. La Nao 71 03730 Javea	0034 966 460 681/Fax: 0034 966 460 681	http://www. cberentals.com email: info@ cberentals.com
	EuroCasa Gestion Inmobiliaria	Aptdo correos 2053 Alicante	0034 655 169 971	email: daniel combret@ yahoo.es
	Sajonia	Avda. Alfonso el Sabio, 16, 8-Izq Alicante	0034 965 230 627/Fax: 0034 965 230 627	email: sajonia21 @yahoo.es
	ServiCasa	C/ Azorin, 4 – Bajo Alicante	0034 965 105 735/Fax: 0034 965 110 5601	http://www. interpisos. com/servicasa email: servicasa3 @hotmail.com

Palma, Majorca

Investor profile:	Retirement, Worker, Holiday, Business		
Category:	A		
Population:	**Total** 320,000		**British** 50,000

Climate:	Hours of sunshine per day in summer	Days of rain per year	Average spring air temp.	Average summer air temp.	Average autumn air temp.	Average winter air temp.	Average water temp.
	11	65	19	29	22	14.5	17

Proximity to:	Airport 7 miles (Palma)	Beach 0.25 miles	Nearest city Palma
Educational facilities:	Number of universities 1	Number of international schools 4	Number of private schools 12
Health services:	Number of public hospitals 1	Number of private hospitals 3	Number of private clinics 4

Shopping:	Number of shopping centres 3	Number of markets 5

Restaurants and bars:	Palma and Portal Nous have lots of highly reputable restaurants and bars. A variety of cuisine is available, including local food (mainly seafood, pork and rice).
Sports and leisure facilities:	Prestigious yacht club. Nightlife at Portal Nous. Cinema showing weekly English-language films. Classical concerts, plays and ballets performed all year round. Annual Chopin festival.

Transport:	**Public transport** Bus service with 22 routes in and around Palma all stopping at Plaza Españato. Trains to Inca and Soller.	**Roads** Main road links from Port de Soller, Port d'Antratx and Manacor. C-713 from Port de Pollenca and Port d'Alcudia.

Crime rate:	High
Main types of employment:	Mostly service sector. Many foreign companies also based in Palma.
Future plans:	Very restricted as already very developed.
Yield range:	28.8%–33.8%

Type of property:	Entry price	Rent – school holiday peak	Rent – peak	Rent – off peak	Average annual yield
2 bed apartment	108,000	1,600	1,280	768	33.8%
3 bed apartment	135,000	1,920	1,536	922	32.4%
3 bed townhouse	202,500	2,560	2,048	1,229	28.8%
Villa	237,600	3,360	2,688	1,613	32.2%

Demand for letting:	School holiday peak High	Peak High	Off peak High

Finance and leisure scores:	Financial (out of 5) 5	Leisure (out of 5) 5	Total (out of 10) 10

Flights scheduled from:	Gatwick, Luton, Stansted, Norwich, Southampton, Bournemouth, Exeter, Bristol, Cardiff, Birmingham, East Midlands, Manchester, Liverpool, Leeds/Bradford, Humberside, Teesside, Newcastle, Glasgow, Glasgow Prestwick, Edinburgh, Aberdeen.

Typical cost of flights:	School holiday peak £115–470	Peak £85–348	Off peak £64–261

Operators:	Air Europa, BMI, Iberia, BA, Air-Berlin, Easyjet, My Travel, Futura, Thomas Cook, Excel Airways, Britannia Airways, Monarch, Air Europa, Air2000, Flyjet.

Description:	Palma is the capital city of Majorca – the largest island of the Balearics, situated 93 miles off the east coast of mainland Spain. Palma is located on the coast within the Bay of Palma and over half of the island's population are believed to live there.
	The city is lively, cosmopolitan and English is widely spoken. Sights to see include the Royal Palace (La Almudaina), a Gothic castle (Castillo de Bellver) and a limestone cathedral (la Seo).
	The cost of living is high but this also assumes a higher quality of life. This is bourne out by the high rental values which have led to the astronomical yields possible. Don't think these yields will last forever. Prices will adjust which will bring down these yields by around half, so don't hang about – buy while its cheap!
	Unemployment rates are low and therefore job prospects are good. So if you're thinking of moving over for good and you happily tend to the services industry then you'll never be short of a job. Prospects are also good for the professional sector as there has been a trend towards these types of companies locating their Spainish branch here.

Hot website:	http://www.mallorcaweb.com/eng/index.html

Estate Agents:	Name	Address	Tel	Web
	David Russell-Pedro Mesquida	Paseo Maritimo 12, 07014 Palma de Mallorca, Mallorca	0034 971 734 073/Fax: 0034 971 451 565	Not disclosed

▶

Estate Agents:	Name	Address	Tel	Web
	Taylor-Woodrow de Espana, S.A.	Calle Aragon 223-223 A, 07008 Palma de Mallorca, Mallorca	0034 971 706 570/Fax: 0034 971 706 565	Not disclosed
	Roberto Jaime Gourlay	Apartado 1423, Palma De Mallorca	0034 971 681 873/Fax: 0034 971 680 320	http://www.mallorca-real-estate.com email: robertog @ocea.es.com/
	Sea Green	Cala Bona Palma de Mallorca	Not disclosed	http://www.mallorca-penthouse.de email: peter@ kerler.de
Letting Agents:	**Name**	**Address**	**Tel**	**Web**
	Europa Inmobiliaria	Antoni Maria Alcover Nº 47 Palma	0034 971 676 787/Fax: 0034 971 676 567	http://www.europa-inmobiliaria. email: europa @europa-inmobiliaria.com
	Arko Inmobiliario	Avda. Son Rapinya, nº 8 1º C, Palma de Mallorca	0034 619 226 688/0034 971 453 689 Fax: 0034 971 457 900	email: arco inmobiliario @hotmail.com

Playa Blanca, Lanzarote

Investor profile:	Retirement, Worker, Holiday, Business
Category:	A

Population:	Total 4,900	British 400

Climate:	Hours of sunshine per day in summer	Days of rain per year	Average spring air temp.	Average summer air temp.	Average autumn air temp.	Average winter air temp.	Average water temp.
	11	57	21	28	24	21	20

Proximity to:	Airport 21 miles (Arrecife)	Beach 0.25 miles	Nearest city 26 miles (Arrecife)

Educational facilities:	Number of universities	Number of international schools	Number of private schools
	0	0	0

Health services:	Number of public hospitals	Number of private hospitals	Number of private clinics
	0	0	1

Shopping:	Number of shopping centres	Number of markets
	1	1

Restaurants and bars:	Seafront fish restaurants, fast food, Mexican, Italian, Chinese, Indian, etc. and local cuisine.
Sports and leisure facilities:	Toninas and Cala Blanca scuba-diving centres. Scuba-diving and windsurfing centres. Sailing cruises. Team Bocinegro big game fishing. Puerto Calero submarine safaris.

Transport:	Public transport Bus services to Arrecife and Teguise market.	Roads Motorway from Arrecife. Also main road from Tias and Teguise.

Crime rate:	Low
Main types of employment:	Tourist sector.
Future plans:	New large sports complex with athletics track and swimming pools (2007). Completion of first marina.
Yield range:	19.5%–21.8%

▶

Type of property:	Entry price	Rent – school holiday peak	Rent – peak	Rent – off peak	Average annual yield
2 bed apartment	106,543	954	763	458	20.4%
3 bed apartment	127,851	1,145	916	550	20.4%
3 bed townhouse	159,814	1,526	1,221	733	21.8%
Villa	234,394	2,003	1,603	962	19.5%

Demand for letting:	School holiday peak High		Peak High		Off peak High

Finance and leisure scores:	Financial (out of 5) 5	Leisure (out of 5) 4	Total (out of 10) 9

Flights scheduled from:	Gatwick, Heathrow, London City, Luton, Stansted, Bristol, Cardiff, Exeter, Newquay, Plymouth, Bournemouth, Southampton, Birmingham, East Midlands, Humberside, Newcastle, Teesside, Blackpool, Isle of Man, Liverpool, Manchester, Aberdeen, Edinburgh, Glasgow, Inverness, Prestwick, Belfast City, Belfast International, Dublin, Guernsey, Jersey, Norwich, Leeds/Bradford.

Typical cost of flights:	School holiday peak £599–834	Peak £444–618	Off peak £333–464

Operators:	BA, SpanAir, Astraeus, Thomas Cook, Monarch, My Travel, Air 2000, Britannia Airways, Excel Airways.

Description:	Playa Blanca is a relatively peaceful resort located on the south-west coast of Lanzarote. Only recently has the resort become developed with many new hotels and apartments which all seem to be catering for the luxurious end of the market.

The three beaches all have bright sands which is making Playa Blanca the choice of many to settle in. At present the resort offers a limited choice of restaurants and shopping but this will all change in 5 years. There is already substantial committed funds from the private sector to make this area a playground for the rich. There will be several Casinos, upmarket bars and clubs, several five star hotels with a la carte menus all landing by 2008.

Yields are fantastic here as property prices are (currently!) cheap and rental prices are healthy. Demand is high for rentals as the area has an all year round season. The island is one of the more easily accessed island compared to the others in its group so there will always be a steady influx of ready and waiting tenants for your property.

Hot website:	http://www.epsylon-dw.com/blanca/

Estate Agents:	Name	Address	Tel	Web
	Enma Consultants and Services	Avda. Papagayo 59, Local 11, Playa Blanca 35570 Yaiza, Lanzarote	0034 928 519 140/Fax: 0034 928 518 995	Not disclosed
	Interval Marketing S.L.	Calle Varadero 4, 35570 Playa Blanca, Lanzarote	0034 928 517 760/Fax: 0034 928 517 762	Not disclosed
	Freedom 4 Sale Spain	Antigua Sala de Proyeccion, Antigua Cine de Teguise, Calle Notes 15, Teguise 35530, Lanzarote	0034 928 845 944/Fax: 0034 928 845 936	http://www. freedom4sale. com/
Letting Agents:	Name	Address	Tel	Web
	Realizaciones Inmobiliarias	Avda. Jablillo, s/n Teguise Canarias, S.A.	0034 928 590 296	Not disclosed

Playa del Ingles, Gran Canaria

Investor profile:	Retirement, Worker, Holiday, Business						
Category:	C						
Population:	Total 4,800				British 500		
Climate:	Hours of sunshine per day in summer	Days of rain per year	Average spring air temp.	Average summer air temp.	Average autumn air temp.	Average winter air temp.	Average water temp.
	11	63	24	26	24	21	20
Proximity to:	Airport 18 miles (Las Palmas)		Beach 0.25 miles		Nearest city 35 miles (Las Palmas)		
Educational facilities:	Number of universities 0		Number of international schools 0		Number of private schools 1		
Health services:	Number of public hospitals 0		Number of private hospitals 0		Number of private clinics 5		
Shopping:	Number of shopping centres 1				Number of markets 1		
Restaurants and bars:	Large amount of restaurants, serving mainly fast food and British food.						
Sports and leisure facilities:	3 golf courses. 5 marinas with variety of watersports. Aquasur waterpark. Palmitos Parque bird gardens and Sioux city wild west theme show nearby.						
Transport:	**Public transport** SALCAI bus service to most of island. Direct bus links to other resorts in south. No rail system.			**Roads** Motorway to south along east coast. Motorways to Trasmontana and Tarifa Alta.			
Crime rate:	Medium						
Main types of employment:	Mainly self-employment e.g. owning bars/shops. Otherwise limited to tourist and service sectors.						
Future plans:	New golf courses and shopping centres.						
Yield range:	6.0%–7.1%						

Type of property:	Entry price	Rent – school holiday peak	Rent – peak	Rent – off peak	Average annual yield
2 bed apartment	110,500	343	274	165	7.1%
3 bed apartment	138,125	412	329	198	6.8%
3 bed townhouse	207,188	549	439	263	6.0%
Villa	243,100	720	576	346	6.8%

Demand for letting:	School holiday peak High		Peak High		Off peak Medium

Finance and leisure scores:	Financial (out of 5) 3	Leisure (out of 5) 4	Total (out of 10) 7

Flights scheduled from:	Gatwick, Heathrow, London City, Luton, Stansted, Bristol, Cardiff, Exeter, Newquay, Plymouth, Bournemouth, Southampton, Birmingham, East Midlands, Humberside, Newcastle, Teesside, Blackpool, Isle of Man, Liverpool, Manchester, Aberdeen, Edinburgh, Glasgow, Inverness, Prestwick, Belfast City, Belfast International, Cork, Dublin, Shannon, Guernsey, Jersey, Norwich, Leeds/Bradford.

Typical cost of flights:	School holiday peak £286–1,278	Peak £212–947	Off peak £159–710

Operators:	Iberia, Air Europa, BA, SpanAir, Astraeus, My Travel, Britannia Airways, Air2000, Excel Airways, Monarch, Thomas Cook.

Description:	Playa del Ingles lies on the south east coast of Gran Canaria. The resort is the biggest and liveliest on the island, with a huge choice of bars, restaurants, pubs and nightclubs and busy beaches stretched over 10 miles. This area has the best climate on the island and also has quite a strong breeze so its popular with the windsurfers.

On the beachfront lies a long, palm-fringed promenade. It has quite a strong nightclub scene and many of the clubs go on in to daybreak. You can guess that it is popular with the younger generations. The resort can get very crowded during the Summer so demand for rental properties will always exist.

Considering the climate is warm all year round a good strategy would be to rent the property during school peak, peak and part off-peak and then enjoy the rest! The island is not difficult to get to and bargain flights can be had off the internet if you book well in advance and fly in the off-peak times.

Hot website:	http://www.red2000.com/spain/canarias/g-canari/

Estate Agents:	Name	Address	Tel	Web
	Fuerteventura Living	Venezuela 8, Officina 7, 35110 Vecindario, Gran Canaria	0034 654 550 076/Fax: 0034 615 029 110	Not disclosed

Estate Agents:	Name	Address	Tel	Web
	RE/MAX Maspalomas S.L.	Avda. Tirajana s/n Playa del Inglés Gran Canaria	0034 928 765 066/Fax: 0034 928 773 250	http://www. katyroque.com email: maspalomas @remax.es
	Freedom 4 Sale Spain	Antigua Sala de Proyeccion, Antigua Cine de Teguise, Calle Notes 15, Teguise 35530, Lanzarote	0034 928 845 944/Fax: 0034 928 845 936	http://www. freedom4sale. com/
	Canarias Estates	Avda. Tirajana 37, Ed. Mercurio 2, 7C, 35100 Playa del Ingles, Gran Canaria	0034 928 761 159/Fax: 0034 928 776 992	http://www. canariasestates. com/ email: canesta@ terra.es
Letting Agents:	Name	Address	Tel	Web
	Canarias Estates	Avda. Tirajana 37, Ed. Mercurio 2, 7C, 35100 Playa del Ingles, Gran Canaria	0034 928 761 159/Fax: 0034 928 776 992	http://www. canariasestates. com/ email: canesta@ terra.es
	Gestion Inmobiliaria Mercacentro	Victor Jara (C.C. Mercacentro) 35110 Vecindario Gran Canaria	Tel/Fax: 0034 928 758 111 Mob: 0034 639 216 866	http://www. inmobiliaria mercacentro .com/ email: merca-inmobiliaria@ terra.com
	RAO Estate	C/ Botánico, Local 57, 35100 San Fernando de Maspalomas Gran Canaria	0034 639 778 338/Fax: 0034 928 764 837	http://www. raoestate.com/ email: info@ raoestate.com
	Grupo Vesua, S.L.	C/ Drago, 48 Gáldar Gran Canaria	0034 928 897 105/Fax: 0034 928 551 153	http:// viviendasen canarias.com/ vesua/

Puerto del Carmen, Lanzarote

Investor profile:	Retirement, Worker, Holiday, Business					
Category:	C					
Population:	**Total** 5,000			**British** 350		
Climate:	Hours of sunshine per day in summer	Days of rain per year	Average spring air temp.	Average summer air temp.	Average autumn air temp.	Average winter air temp.	Average water temp.
	10	57	21	28	24	21	20

Proximity to:	**Airport** 6 miles (Arrecife)	**Beach** 0.25 miles	**Nearest city** 9 miles (Arrecife)
Educational facilities:	**Number of universities** 0	**Number of international schools** 0	**Number of private schools** 0
Health services:	**Number of public hospitals** 0	**Number of private hospitals** 0	**Number of private clinics** 4

Shopping:	**Number of shopping centres** 0	**Number of markets** 2
Restaurants and bars:	Fast-food, Mexican, Italian, Chinese, Indian, etc. and also local cuisine. Live music bars in La Avendida Maritima and El Centro Atlantico. Quieter bars in Vardero.	
Sports and leisure facilities:	Ana Segunda sport fishing. 3 scuba-diving centres. Deep-sea fishing. Horse-riding and golf courses in nearby towns. Parascending club. Tamaran and Megafun jeep safari tours. Rancho Texas Park with attractions and animals. Casino. Classical music concerts and recitals in old town.	
Transport:	**Public transport** Bus services to Teguise market and Arrecife, where you can get connecting buses to rest of island.	**Roads** Motorway from Playa Blanca. Also main road from north of island.
Crime rate:	Low	
Main types of employment:	Tourist sector.	
Future plans:	Limited to preserve nature.	
Yield range:	7.5%–8.8%	

Type of property:	Entry price	Rent – school holiday peak	Rent – peak	Rent – off peak	Average annual yield
2 bed apartment	172,000	663	530	318	8.8%
3 bed apartment	215,000	796	636	382	8.4%
3 bed townhouse	322,500	1,061	849	509	7.5%
Villa	378,400	1,392	1,114	668	8.4%

Demand for letting:	School holiday peak High	Peak High	Off peak High

Finance and leisure scores:	Financial (out of 5) 3	Leisure (out of 5) 4	Total (out of 10) 7

Flights scheduled from:	Gatwick, Heathrow, London City, Luton, Stansted, Bristol, Cardiff, Exeter, Newquay, Plymouth, Bournemouth, Southampton, Birmingham, East Midlands, Humberside, Newcastle, Teesside, Blackpool, Isle of Man, Liverpool, Manchester, Aberdeen, Edinburgh, Glasgow, Inverness, Prestwick, Belfast City, Belfast International, Dublin, Guernsey, Jersey, Norwich, Leeds/Bradford.

Typical cost of flights:	School holiday peak £599–834	Peak £444–618	Off peak £333–464

Operators:	BA, SpanAir, Astraeus, Thomas Cook, Monarch, My Travel, Air 2000, Britannia Airways, Excel Airways.

Description:	Puerto del Carmen is a resort situated near the capital of Lanzarote, Arrecife. It is the largest and liveliest resort on the island with several beaches stretched over 3 miles, a variety of shops and a thriving nightlife. As well as having a golden sandy beach there is also an old town which has plenty to see.
	This area enjoys a mild dry climate all year round so it is always in demand – both from people wishing to live here and from people wishing to holiday here. It is particularly popular with young singles and couples. There is an established long term rental market so this area would suit anyone wishing to buy a home with the intention of residing in it in the future, say 5 to 10 years away.
	The local property market is healthy and the area is constantly being developed. However this should soon reach a peak so demand for new properties will be high.

Hot website:	http://www.lanzarote.com/

Estate Agents:	Name	Address	Tel	Web
	Cactus Consulting	Calle Juan Carlos 1,26, C.C. la Curva, Local 2, Puerto del Carmen, Lanzarote	0034 928 515 184/Fax: 0034 928 512 202	Not disclosed

Estate Agents:	Name	Address	Tel	Web
	Inversiones Timanfaya Real Estate	Avda. De al Playas 1–L2A, 35510 Puerto del Carmen, Lanzarote	0034 928 596 220/Fax: 0034 928 514 801	Not disclosed
	Freedom 4 Sale Spain	Antigua Sala de Proyeccion, Antigua Cine de Teguise, Calle Notes 15, Teguise 35530, Lanzarote	0034 928 845 944/Fax: 0034 928 845 936	http://www. freedom4sale. com/
Letting Agents:	Name	Address	Tel	Web
	Realizaciones Inmobiliarias	Avda. Jablillo, s/n Teguise Canarias	0034 928 590 296	Not disclosed
	RAO Estate	C/ Botánico, Local 57, 35100 San Fernando de Maspalomas Gran Canaria	0034 639 778 338/Fax: 0034 928 764 837	http://www. raoestate.com/ email: info@ raoestate.com
	Grupo Vesua, S.L.	C/ Drago, 48 Gáldar Gran Canaria	0034 928 897 105/Fax: 0034 928 551 153	http:// viviendasen canarias.com/ vesua/

Puerto de la Cruz, Tenerife

Investor profile:	Retirement, Worker, Holiday, Business						
Category:	A						
Population:	**Total** 27,436				**British** 2,000		
Climate:	Hours of sunshine per day in summer	Days of rain per year	Average spring air temp.	Average summer air temp.	Average autumn air temp.	Average winter air temp.	Average water temp.
	11	33	21.5	27	24	20	21
Proximity to:	**Airport** 62 miles (Reina Sofia)		**Beach** 0.25 miles		**Nearest city** 24 miles (Santa Cruz)		
Educational facilities:	Number of universities 0		Number of international schools 1		Number of private schools 3		
Health services:	Number of public hospitals 0		Number of private hospitals 2		Number of private clinics 23		
Shopping:	Number of shopping centres 2				Number of markets 0		
Restaurants and bars:	International cuisine widely available. Also fast food.						
Sports and leisure facilities:	Man-made swimming pool complex with seven pools. Selection of beaches nearby. Scuba-diving courses. Surfing beach. Oratava Valley national park inland. Public sports centre with indoor swimming pool. Tennis clubs. Annual season of classical music concerts. Loro Park theme park (a Thailand styled tropical paradise) with sea-life aquarium and parrot aviaries. Risco Bello Aquatic Gardens and Casino at Taoro Park. Botanical Park at La Paz. Archaeological museum in town.						
Transport:	**Public transport** Frequent bus services (run by TITSA) across island's main roads.			**Roads** Motorways from Santa Cruz.			
Crime rate:	Medium						
Main types of employment:	Mainly tourist and service sectors.						
Future plans:	Extension of motorway.						
Yield range:	10.1%–11.8%						

Type of property:	Entry price	Rent – school holiday peak	Rent – peak	Rent – off peak	Average annual yield
2 bed apartment	148,000	769	615	369	11.8%
3 bed apartment	185,000	923	738	443	11.4%
3 bed townhouse	277,500	1,230	984	591	10.1%
Villa	325,600	1,615	1,292	775	11.3%

Demand for letting:	School holiday peak High	Peak High	Off peak High

Finance and leisure scores:	Financial (out of 5) 5	Leisure (out of 5) 4	Total (out of 10) 9

Flights scheduled from:	Gatwick, Heathrow, London City, Luton, Stansted, Bristol, Cardiff, Exeter, Newquay, Plymouth, Bournemouth, Southampton, Birmingham, East Midlands, Humberside, Newcastle, Teesside, Blackpool, Isle of Man, Liverpool, Manchester, Aberdeen, Edinburgh, Glasgow, Inverness, Prestwick, Belfast City, Belfast International, Dublin, Guernsey, Jersey, Norwich, Leeds/Bradford.

Typical cost of flights:	School holiday peak £154–464	Peak £114–344	Off peak £86–258

Operators:	Monarch, Iberia, Air Europa, BA, BMI, Flyjet, Air2000, Thomas Cook, Astraeus, Britannia Airways, LTE International, My Travel, Excel Airways, Futura.

Description:	Puerto de la Cruz is a cosmopolitan city and is the main tourist resort on the north coast of Tenerife. Inland from the resort the land is lush compared to the south.
	It is a popular place for owning a holiday home. Houses in this area tend to be large with gardens and command a high price. The yields are healthy due to higher rents achievable which reflect the desirability of this resort.
	This area is considered to be the more affluent part of Tenerife. There are many classical concerts throughout the year which attract a different type of clientele. Its quite a journey to get here, being 62 miles from the airport, but this preserves its exclusivity.
	The climate is what you would expect from Tenerife being neither too hot or too cold all year round. Using your holiday home throughout the year is possible, as is renting the property out. If you can stall using your home then its worth considering a long term let for 1 year or more. There is big demand for long term lets and tenants are willing to pay a premium for this thus further enhancing your yields.

Hot website:	http://www.eurosol.com/

Estate Agents:	Name	Address	Tel	Web
	Concay Immo	Edf. Iguazu, Apartado de Correos 670, 38400 Puerto de la Cruz, Tenerife	0034 922 371 452/Fax: 0034 922 372 106	Not disclosed
	Freedom 4 Sale Spain	Antigua Sala de Proyeccion, Antigua Cine de Teguise, Calle Notes 15, Teguise 35530, Lanzarote	0034 928 845 944/Fax: 0034 928 845 936	http://www. freedom4sale. com/
	The Horizon Property Group S.L.	Not disclosed	0161 476 0666 01384 866000	http://www. horizonproperty group.com/
	Eurosol	First Link CC Teide – Local 5 San Eugenio Alto Adeje 38660 Tenerife	0034 922 715 661/Fax: 0034 922 715 953	http://www. eurosol.com/
Letting Agents:	Name	Address	Tel	Web
	Eurosol	First Link CC Teide – Local 5 San Eugenio Alto Adeje 38660 Tenerife	0034 922 715 661/Fax: 0034 922 715 953	http://www. eurosol.com/
	Astliz Estate Agents	P.O.Box 135 Los Gigantes 38683 Santiago del Teide S/C de Tenerife	0034 922 796 776/Fax: 0034 922 796 973	http://www. canaryislands- internet.com/ email: info@ canarian-villas. com

Playa d'en Bossa, Ibiza

Investor profile:	Retirement, Worker, Holiday, Business
Category:	C

Population:	Total	British
	8,000	1,000

Climate:	Hours of sunshine per day in summer	Days of rain per year	Average spring air temp.	Average summer air temp.	Average autumn air temp.	Average winter air temp.	Average water temp.
	11	40	15	25	20	12	17

Proximity to:	Airport	Beach	Nearest city
	1 mile (Ibiza)	0.25 miles	2 miles (Ibiza Town)

Educational facilities:	Number of universities	Number of international schools	Number of private schools
	0	0	0

Health services:	Number of public hospitals	Number of private hospitals	Number of private clinics
	0	0	1

Shopping:	Number of shopping centres	Number of markets
	0	1

Restaurants and bars:	Predominantly fast food, takeaways and British food. Many bars.
Sports and leisure facilities:	Water-skiing and windsurfing schools. Tennis clubs. Aguamar water-park open during summer only. Hillbilly hoedown wild west shows. Bowling centre with amusement arcade. Big nightclub, Space (opens at 6am).

Transport:	Public transport	Roads
	Frequent bus service to other resorts and main towns. Night bus (Discobus) between resort and main nightclubs during summer.	Main roads from San Antonio and Sant Joan.

Crime rate:	High
Main types of employment:	Mostly tourist sector during Summer.
Future plans:	None.
Yield range:	6.7%–7.8%

Type of property:	Entry price	Rent – school holiday peak	Rent – peak	Rent – off peak	Average annual yield
2 bed apartment	215,800	742	594	356	7.8%
3 bed apartment	269,750	890	712	427	7.5%
3 bed townhouse	404,625	1,187	950	570	6.7%
Villa	474,760	1,558	1,247	748	7.5%

Demand for letting:	School holiday peak High		Peak High		Off peak Low

Finance and leisure scores:	Financial (out of 5) 3	Leisure (out of 5) 3	Total (out of 10) 6

Flights scheduled from:	Gatwick, Heathrow, London City, Luton, Stansted, Bristol, Cardiff, Exeter, Newquay, Plymouth, Bournemouth, Southampton, Birmingham, East Midlands, Humberside, Newcastle, Teesside, Blackpool, Isle of Man, Liverpool, Manchester, Aberdeen, Edinburgh, Glasgow, Inverness, Prestwick, Belfast City, Belfast International, Dublin, Guernsey, Jersey, Norwich, Leeds/Bradford.

Typical cost of flights:	School holiday peak £282–1,025	Peak £209–759	Off peak £154–571

Operators:	SpanAir, Air Europa, Monarch, Air France, Britannia Airways, My travel, Astraeus, Iberworld, Thomas Cook, Air 2000, Excel Airways.

Description:	Playa d'en Bossa is a large, purpose-built resort and suburb located south of the capital. It consists of hotels and apartments surrounding one palm-lined main street, with a lively nightlife atmostphere.

It also has Ibiza's longest blue-flag sandy beach. Although there are no public or private hospitals in the area there are several public health centres.

Property is expensive here but its expensive everywhere in Ibiza! Playa d'en Bossa can be one of the cheaper alternatives to other areas in the island. The rental demand is strong only in the peak seasons as the temperature drops significantly in the winter. But the rent is sufficient in these peak times to cover the voids in the winter and much more.

This area is one of the few places in Ibiza where it is suitable for all the family. Ibiza is THE island of Spain and will be for the next 20 years. Your investment is safe here as there will always be a ready rental and resale market for your property.

One drawback of the area is that not only does Ibiza attract holidaymakers it also attracts the thieves! Ibiza is addressing this problem and there is now a stronger police presence. Spain understand that this island is the jewel in their crown and they will do whatever it takes to protect it.

Hot website:	http://www.ibiza-spotlight.com/

Estate Agents:	Name	Address	Tel	Web
	Fincas Eivissa	Carretera Ibiza San José Kilómetro 1,5 Apart Can Bellotera	0034 639 694 469/Fax: 0034 971 398 185	http://www. fincaseivissa. com/ email: fincas eivissa@inter book.net
	Interealty Balearics	Plaza Santa Ponsa, 4 Local 1 en E-07180, Santa Ponsa, Mallorca	0034 971 699 545/Fax: 0034 971 699 556	www.interealty-mallorca.com
	Inmobiliaria Villa Contact	Paseo. S'Alamera 14, 07840 Santa Eulalia del Rio Ibiza	0034 971 330 374/331 554 Fax: 0034 971 330 458	http://www. villacontact. com/ email: info@ villacontact.com
	BBS Consulting Raimund Schreck-Heuer	Avda. Es Cubells 1, Edificio S'Atalaya, Bajos F Apdo. 164 E-07830 San José, Ibiza	0034 971 800 705/Fax: 0034 971 800 664 Mob: 0034 649 190 465	http://www. bbs-ibiza.com/ eng/index_en. htm email: bbs@ctv. es
Letting Agents:	Name	Address	Tel	Web
	Houseland-co-ibiza	Unknown	0034 971 318 539	http://www. houseland-co-ibiza.com/ingles /principal.htm email: info@ house-co-ibiza.com

Playa de las Americas, Tenerife

Investor profile:	Retirement, Worker, Holiday, Business						
Category:	C						

Population:	Total 6,700				British 1,000		

Climate:	Hours of sunshine per day in summer	Days of rain per year	Average spring air temp.	Average summer air temp.	Average autumn air temp.	Average winter air temp.	Average water temp.
	11	33	21.5	27	24	20	21

Proximity to:	Airport 11 miles (Reina Sofia)	Beach 0.25 miles	Nearest city 46 miles (Santa Cruz)

Educational facilities:	Number of universities 0	Number of international schools 1	Number of private schools 1

Health services:	Number of public hospitals 0	Number of private hospitals 1	Number of private clinics 5

Shopping:	Number of shopping centres 2	Number of markets 1

Restaurants and bars:	Mostly British food and fast food.
Sports and leisure facilities:	Sailing. Scuba-diving courses. La Troya, Conquistador and Fatenia surfing beaches. Windsurfing at Fatenia. Skateboarding ramps. 10 pin bowling alley. Hang-gliding club. Adeje, Los Cristianos and Los Palos golf courses nearby. Casino. Octopus Aquapark with sun bathing areas, slides, tubes, pools, diving boards, dolphins shows. Many nightclubs in Veronicas area.

Transport:	**Public transport** Frequent bus services (run by TITSA) across island's main roads.	**Roads** Motorways from Santa Cruz.

Crime rate:	Low
Main types of employment:	Mainly tourist and service sectors. Many foreign companies based in and around the resort.
Future plans:	Addition of more 4 and 5 star hotels. New cinema complex.
Yield range:	7.6%–8.9%

Type of property:	Entry price	Rent – school holiday peak	Rent – peak	Rent – off peak	Average annual yield
2 bed apartment	142,300	558	446	268	8.9%
3 bed apartment	177,875	670	536	321	8.6%
3 bed townhouse	266,813	893	714	429	7.6%
Villa	313,060	1,172	937	562	8.5%

Demand for letting:	School holiday peak High	Peak High	Off peak High

Finance and leisure scores:	Financial (out of 5) 4	Leisure (out of 5) 4	Total (out of 10) 8

Flights scheduled from:	Gatwick, Heathrow, London City, Luton, Stansted, Bristol, Cardiff, Exeter, Newquay, Plymouth, Bournemouth, Southampton, Birmingham, East Midlands, Humberside, Newcastle, Teesside, Blackpool, Isle of Man, Liverpool, Manchester, Aberdeen, Edinburgh, Glasgow, Inverness, Prestwick, Belfast City, Belfast International, Dublin, Guernsey, Jersey, Norwich, Leeds/Bradford.

Typical cost of flights:	School holiday peak £154–464	Peak £114–344	Off peak £86–258

Operators:	Monarch, Iberia, Air Europa, BA, BMI, Flyjet, Air2000, Thomas Cook, Astraeus, Britannia Airways, LTE International, My Travel, Excel Airways, Futura.

Description:	Tenerife is the largest of the Canary Islands, and Playa de las Americas is Tenerife's largest and most developed resort, situated on the south-west coast of the island. There is lively nightlife and a variety of leisure activities. If you like lively holidays then this may be the perfect place to invest as there is plenty to do in the day, evening and early hours of the morning! One thing that is noticeable in the past few years is that this area is going more upmarket. There seems to be a demand for better quality hotels as Tenerife is establishing itself as being one of the better islands in Spain. This will attract a better type of holidaymaker. If you can get a property near the beach or up in the hills then you'll have no trouble letting it out and you can afford to be fussy over who you have as tenants. Capital growth is likely due to the influx of investment in this area. The movement upwards of the area's image is helping push up demand for properties so be quick!

Hot website:	http://www.eurosol.com/

Estate Agents:	Name	Address	Tel	Web
	The Property Gallery	C.C. Centro Playa Local 9, Purto Colon San Eugenio Bajo, Playa de Las Americas, 38660 Adeje, Tenerife	0034 922 719 925/Fax: 0034 922 719 616	Not disclosed
	Sunway Tenerife	Parque Cattleya 2, Playa de Las Americas, Tenerife	0034 922 790 021/Fax: 0034 922 795 172	Not disclosed
	Tenerife Property Shop	Local 117, Puerto Colon, Playa de Las Americas, Tenerife	0034 922 714 700/Fax: 0034 922 715 720	Not disclosed
	Urban Americas	Centro Comercial Oasis Dakota No. 18, Calle Helsinki, Fanabe, Costa Adeje, Tenerife	0034 922 719 617/Fax: 0034 922 719 621	Not disclosed

Letting Agents:	Name	Address	Tel	Web
	Visaverde CS S.L.	Garden City, Playa de Las Americas, Tenerife	0034 922 794 214/Fax: 0034 922 796 171	http://www. visaverde.com email: info@ visaverde.com
	Leisure Estates International	Fountain Court High Street Market Harborough Leicestershire LE16 7AF	0870 870 8850 Fax: 01858 433 266	http://www. leisure-estates.co.uk/ email: sales@ leisure-estates. co.uk
	Eurosol	First Link CC Teide – Local 5 San Eugenio Alto Adeje 38660 Tenerife	0034 922 715 661/Fax: 0034 922 715 953	http://www. eurosol.com/
	Astliz Estate Agents	P.O. Box 135 Los Gigantes 38683 Santiago del Teide S/C de Tenerife	0034 922 796 776/Fax: 0034 922 796 973	http://www. canaryislands-internet.com/ email: info@ canarian-villas. com

Roquetas de Mar, Costa de Almeria

Investor profile:	Retirement, Worker, Holiday, Business		
Category:	C		
Population:	Total 53,360		British 2,000

Climate:	Hours of sunshine per day in summer	Days of rain per year	Average spring air temp.	Average summer air temp.	Average autumn air temp.	Average winter air temp.	Average water temp.
	11	7	20	30	22	16	20

Proximity to:	Airport 15 miles (Almeria)	Beach 0.25 miles	Nearest city 15 miles (Almeria)
Educational facilities:	Number of universities	Number of international schools	Number of private schools
	0	0	1
Health services:	Number of public hospitals	Number of private hospitals	Number of private clinics
	0	0	7

Shopping:	Number of shopping centres	Number of markets
	1	2

Restaurants and bars:	Local, English and Italian restaurants as well as international cuisine all available. Choice of cocktail and disco bars.
Sports and leisure facilities:	Playa Serena 18-hole golf course. Tennis courts. Horse-riding stables. Sailing, waterskiing and windsurfing schools. Biking tours. Rowing club. Mariopark water-park open in Summer. Cabo de Gata and Las Albuferas de Adra national parks nearby.

Transport:	Public transport Limited bus services from Almeria.	Roads N-340 from Costa del Sol/Malaga. N-324 motorway from Granada.

Crime rate:	Low
Main types of employment:	Agriculture and tourism.
Future plans:	Government's Excellence Plan – expansion towards Aguadulce resort, including sports pavilion, large shopping centre, casino, thousands of new homes, theatre and aquarium. Also new music school, bullring and open air amphitheatre.
Yield range:	6.6%–7.7%

Type of property:	Entry price	Rent – school holiday peak	Rent – peak	Rent – off peak	Average annual yield
2 bed apartment	147,502	499	399	240	7.7%
3 bed apartment	184,378	599	479	287	7.4%
3 bed townhouse	276,566	798	639	383	6.6%
Villa	324,504	1,048	838	503	7.4%

Demand for letting:	School holiday peak High	Peak Medium	Off peak Medium

Finance and leisure scores:	Financial (out of 5) 3	Leisure (out of 5) 3	Total (out of 10) 6

Flights scheduled from:	Gatwick, Heathrow, Luton, Stansted, Bristol, Cardiff, Birmingham, East Midlands, Newcastle, Teesside, Liverpool, Manchester, Leeds/Bradford, Glasgow, Inverness, Belfast International, Dublin.

Typical cost of flights:	School holiday peak £259–828	Peak £192–613	Off peak £144–460

Operators:	Iberia, BA, BMI, European Air Charter, Thomas Cook, Monarch, Air 2000, Britannia Airways, Excel Airways, My Travel.

Description:	Roquetas de Mar is the largest resort in Costa de Almeria, specialising in package holidays. The resort developed from a typical fishing village which still exists. It has a number of long sandy beaches (including a naturist beach!) and a harbour. Sights to see in the town include the Roman statue of Dionysius, the preserved amphitheatre Cerro de Villavieja, and the ruins of the castles of Santa Ana and Los Bajos. Property is on the whole cheaper than on the Costa del Sol, but prices have risen steadily over the past few years. This is expected to continue for quite some time as the resort is the fastest growing town in the province of Almeria. Roquetas de Mar is also planned to host part of the 2005 Mediterranean Games. Even though the yields are not that exciting, the opportunity for capital growth is. There has been and will be significant investment from the private and governmental sector till at least 2007. The government has ear-marked this area as one of it's flagship areas to promote Spain to the rest of the world. The private sector has followed through with investment accordingly. If you want a holiday home that offers you more than just the standard holiday facilities then this area could be right for you. It will become a resort than pines to be a city!

Hot website:	http://www.info-roquetas.com/

Estate Agents:	Name	Address	Tel	Web
	Casas Almeria	Urb. Costa Fleming, 04600 Huercal Overa, Almeria	0034 636 101 208/Fax: 0034 950 134 434	Not disclosed

Estate Agents:	Name	Address	Tel	Web
	Home4home property consultants	The Lodga, Piedra Amarilla, 04810 Partaloa, Almeria	0034 660 232 894	Not disclosed
	Indarko Expertos Inmobiliarios	Avda. Playa Serena, s/n-Edif. Roquetas de Mar	0034 950 627 007/Fax: 0034 950 627 157	http://www. indarko.com email: indarko@ wanadoo.es
	Almerisol	Avda. Mediterraneo 99 Roquetas de Mar	0034 950 333 680/Fax: 0034 950 333 680	http://www. almerisol-info. com email: main@ almerisol- info.com

Letting Agents:	Name	Address	Tel	Web
	Almeria In The Sun	Jose Jerez, Cabrera Sales Office, Cortijo Cabrera, Aptdo. Correos 17, Almeria	01708 721919/ 01708 374467	enquiries@ almeriain thesun.com
	ARCO Alquileres y venta	Avda. Playa Serena – Edf. Las Garzas, bl. 4, local 3 E-04740 Roquetas de Mar	0034 950 334 224	http://www. arco-roquetas. com/ email: arco_ roquetas@hot mail.com
	Complete Management Service – Roquetas de Mar	Not disclosed	0034 950 334 614/Fax: 0034 950 334 498	email: info@ cms-propertys. com
	Mediterra Inmobiliaria	Dársena 1 – Local 3 Pto. Deportivo Almerimar 04700 El Ejido – Almería	0034 950 497 960	http://www. mediterraspain. com/ email: info@ mediterra spain.com

Salou, Costa Dorada

Investor profile:	Retirement, Worker, Holiday, Business
Category:	B

Population:	Total 16,000	British 500

Climate:	Hours of sunshine per day in summer	Days of rain per year	Average spring air temp.	Average summer air temp.	Average autumn air temp.	Average winter air temp.	Average water temp.
	9	102	17	27	24	12	19

Proximity to:	Airport 9.3 miles (Reus)	Beach 0.25 miles	Nearest city 7.5 miles (Tarragona)

Educational facilities:	Number of universities	Number of international schools	Number of private schools
	0	0	4

Health services:	Number of public hospitals	Number of private hospitals	Number of private clinics
	0	2	3

Shopping:	Number of shopping centres	Number of markets
	0	2

Restaurants and bars:	Over 100 restaurants in the area. Predominantly fast food and international cuisine. Over 70 bars/pubs.
Sports and leisure facilities:	Watersports such as jet-skiing, water-skiing, kayaking, sailing, parasailing and windsurfing at Paseo Maritimo promenade/Platja Llevant beach. Boat excursions along coastline. Funfair and amusement arcades. 3 nearby golf courses. Go-kart track. Universal Studios, Port Aventura and Aqualeon theme parks. Aquopolis water park 6 km along coast. 8 nightclubs.

Transport:	**Public transport** Train services from Barcelona, Salou, Tarragona and Valencia. Local and regional bus services.	**Roads** A-7 motorway from Calafell to southern Costa Dorada. A-16 from Castelldefels (near Barcelona) to Calafell. N-340 single-carriageway along coast.

Crime rate:	Low
Main types of employment:	Mainly tourist sector.
Future plans:	New residential constructions. New yacht club. New coastal route following coves of Cape Salou. Urban planning project – modernise infrastructure and re-zone territory.

Yield range:	11.3%–11.9%				
Type of property:	Entry price	Rent – school holiday peak	Rent – peak	Rent – off peak	Average annual yield
2 bed apartment	147,725	770	616	370	11.9%
3 bed apartment	177,271	924	739	444	11.9%
3 bed townhouse	221,588	1,232	986	591	12.7%
Villa	324,997	1,617	1,294	776	11.3%

Demand for letting:	School holiday peak High	Peak High	Off peak Medium

Finance and leisure scores:	Financial (out of 5) 4	Leisure (out of 5) 4	Total (out of 10) 8

Flights scheduled from:	Gatwick, Heathrow, Luton, Stansted, Bristol, Cardiff, Birmingham, East Midlands, Newcastle, Teesside, Liverpool, Manchester, Leeds/Bradford, Glasgow, Inverness, Belfast International, Dublin.

Typical cost of flights:	School holiday peak £116–235	Peak £86–174	Off peak £65–131

Operators:	Monarch, Air 2000, Thomas Cook, Britannia Airways, BA, Excel Airways, My Travel.

Description:	Salou is a lively and modern tourist resort, popular with both British and Spanish families and couples. It has a palm tree-lined promenade parallel to the beach, along with coves. It has recently undergone remodelling to make it more attractive. There are 8 beaches in total stretching over 4 kms. The Salvador Dali museum is situated in nearby Figueres and there are also the historical towns of Tarragona and Altafulla nearby. I have chosen this place as there seems to be a lot happening here. It offers more than your average Spainish resort. A major regeneration programme has been undertaken so the popularity of the area will increase. Yields are very respectable so a good return can be had here. Flights are cheap to Reus, the local airport, so getting here won't be a problem. There are not many british here but I suspect this will all change. There have been several residential developments springing up and most of the buyers are British. Capital growth is likely but the timescale is uncertain. What you can be certain of is above average yields. For me this makes it a good place to invest as the returns are based on some kind of reality rather than having to gaze into the crystal ball.

Hot website:	http://www.salou.co.uk/

Estate Agents:	Name	Address	Tel	Web
	Costa Dorada Real Estate	Mont Roig del Camp Costa Dorada	0034 977 179 661/Fax: 0034 977 170 876	http://www. costa-dorada- casa-finca.com/ email: info@ dorfmann.com

Estate Agents:	Name	Address	Tel	Web
	Fincas Maritim Playa	Paseo Miramar, 10 Apartado de Correos 244 43840 Salou Tarragona	Tel/Fax: (0034) 977 380 639 – Tel: 0034 977 351 641	http://www. fut.es/~heideh/ email: heideh @tinet.fut.es
	Inmobiliaria Derk Snijders	Passeig de Jaume 1, 10 Edificio Las Acacias, Salou	0034 977 352 781	Not disclosed
	Icas Agencia Inmobiliaria	C / de Barcelona, 16 1º 1º, Salou	0034 977 388 054	Not disclosed
Letting Agents:	**Name**	**Address**	**Tel**	**Web**
	Brisasol	Not disclosed	Not disclosed	http://www. brisasol.es/ central@ brisasol.es
	Universal Holiday Centre	C/ Bruselas, 39 Salou Tarragona	0034 977 530 10/Fax: 0034 977 353 448	http://www. universal holidaycentre. com/indexb. html email: info@ universal holidaycentre. com
	Fincas Maritim Playa	Paseo Miramar, 10 Apartado de Correos 244 43840 Salou Tarragona	Tel/Fax: 0034 977 380 639 – Tel: 0034 977 351 641	http://www. fut.es/~heideh/ email: heideh @tinet.fut.es
	Alquilo Apartamentos	Angelita Sanz De Ayala & Estanislao De Aranzadi Aburto C/Mayor 27, 1º 1ª, Salou 43840	0034 616 294 966 – 0034 670 209 009/Fax: 0034 977 384 628	http://www. alquilo apartamentos salou.com/

San Antonio, Ibiza

Investor profile:	Retirement, Worker, Holiday, Business
Category:	C

Population:	Total	British
	18,000	6,000

Climate:	Hours of sunshine per day in summer	Days of rain per year	Average spring air temp.	Average summer air temp.	Average autumn air temp.	Average winter air temp.	Average water temp.
	11	40	15	25	20	12	17

Proximity to:	Airport	Beach	Nearest city
	14 miles (Ibiza)	0.25 miles	10 miles (Ibiza Town)

Educational facilities:	Number of universities	Number of international schools	Number of private schools
	0	0	0

Health services:	Number of public hospitals	Number of private hospitals	Number of private clinics
	0	0	1

Shopping:	Number of shopping centres	Number of markets
	0	1

Restaurants and bars:	High concentration of restaurants serving variety of international cuisine e.g. traditional Spanish and Ibicenco, Italian, local fish, steaks, grills, Chinese and Indian. Also many bars, including famous Café del Mar, Mambo and the family-orientated Maxims.
Sports and leisure facilities:	Portus Magnus marina with sailing and diving centres. Parasailing and jetskiing at San Antonio bay. Horse-riding stables. Captain Nemo boat trips. Go-karting. Tennis club. Horse racing at Sant Rafel Hippodrome. Aquarium. Expatriate theatre groups and sports clubs. Rodeo Fun Park with leisure activities for children. Buccanero Kid bowling alley. Big nightclubs Eden and Es Paradis in West End. 2 further nightclubs Privilege and Amnesia in Sant Rafel.

Transport:	**Public transport** Frequent local bus service to other resorts and main towns. Night bus (Discobus) between resort and main nightclubs during summer.	**Roads** Main roads from San Antonio and Sant Joan.

Crime rate:	High
Main types of employment:	Mostly tourist sector during Summer.
Future plans:	New golf course.

Yield range:	6.8%–7.9%				
Type of property:	Entry price	Rent – school holiday peak	Rent – peak	Rent – off peak	Average annual yield
2 bed apartment	186,650	650	520	312	7.9%
3 bed apartment	233,313	780	624	374	7.6%
3 bed townhouse	349,969	1,040	832	499	6.8%
Villa	410,630	1,365	1,092	655	7.6%
Demand for letting:	School holiday peak High		Peak High		Off peak Low
Finance and leisure scores:	Financial (out of 5) 3		Leisure (out of 5) 5		Total (out of 10) 8
Flights scheduled from:	Gatwick, Heathrow, London City, Luton, Stansted, Bristol, Cardiff, Exeter, Newquay, Plymouth, Bournemouth, Southampton, Birmingham, East Midlands, Humberside, Newcastle, Teesside, Blackpool, Isle of Man, Liverpool, Manchester, Aberdeen, Edinburgh, Glasgow, Inverness, Prestwick, Belfast City, Belfast International, Dublin, Guernsey, Jersey, Norwich, Leeds/Bradford.				
Typical cost of flights:	School holiday peak £282–1,025		Peak £209–759		Off peak £154–571
Operators:	SpanAir, Air Europa, Monarch, Air France, Britannia Airways, My travel, Astraeus, Iberworld, Thomas Cook, Air 2000, Excel Airways.				
Description:	San Antonio is situated on the west of the island and is the most lively and popular destination on Ibiza, particularly with young adults. The town has 2 main areas: the West End (where the majority of nightlife is located) and the Bay (a port surrounded by huge developments). There is also an old town with some preserved architecture. San Antonio bay has 5 small beaches. The beaches are rocky compared to the east coast, however this makes it ideal for scuba-diving and other watersports. Although there are no public or private hospitals in the area there are several public health centres. There are many high-rise hotel and apartment blocks in the area. Although property in Ibiza is considered to be expensive, apartments in San Antonio are slightly cheaper and offer better value. Like Playa d'en Bossa demand for rental properties is focused on the peak season only but the rental prices are sufficient enough to cover all costs and more. One drawback of the area is that not only does San Antonio attract holidaymakers it also attracts the thieves! Ibiza is addressing this problem and there is now a stronger police presence. Spain understand that this island is the jewel in their crown and they will do whatever it takes to protect it.				
Hot website:	http://www.ibiza-spotlight.com/				

Estate Agents:	Name	Address	Tel	Web
	Fincas Eivissa	Carretera Ibiza San José Kilómetro 1,5 Apart Can Bellotera	0034 639 694 469/Fax: 0034 971 398 185	http://www. fincaseivissa. com/ email: fincas eivissa@inter book.net
	Interealty Balearics	Plaza Santa Ponsa, 4 Local 1 en E-07180, Santa Ponsa, Mallorca	0034 971 699 545/Fax: 0034 971 699 556	www.interealty-mallorca.com
	Inmobiliaria Villa Contact	Paseo. S'Alamera 14, 07840 Santa Eulalia del Rio Ibiza	0034 971 330 374/331 554 Fax: 0034 971 330 458	http://www. villacontact. com/ email: info@ villacontact.com
	BBS Consulting Raimund Schreck-Heuer	Avda. Es Cubells 1, Edificio S'Atalaya, Bajos F Apdo. 164 E-07830 San José Ibiza	0034 971 800 705/Fax: 0034 971 800 664 Mob: 0034 649 190 465	http://www. bbs-ibiza.com/ eng/index_en. htm email: bbs@ctv. es
Letting Agents:	Name	Address	Tel	Web
	Houseland-co-ibiza	Unknown	0034 971 318 539	http://www. houseland-co-ibiza.com/ingles /principal.htm email: info@ house-co-ibiza.com

San Sebastian, Basque Country

Investor profile:	Retirement, Worker, Holiday, Business		
Category:	C		

Population:	Total 180,000	British 2,000

Climate:	Hours of sunshine per day in summer	Days of rain per year	Average spring air temp.	Average summer air temp.	Average autumn air temp.	Average winter air temp.	Average water temp.
	8	175	18	25	20	14	15

Proximity to:	Airport 62.5 miles (Bilbao)	Beach 0.25–2 miles	Nearest city San Sebastian

Educational facilities:	Number of universities	Number of international schools	Number of private schools
	1	0	2

Health services:	Number of public hospitals	Number of private hospitals	Number of private clinics
	1	1	7

Shopping:	Number of shopping centres	Number of markets
	3	4

Restaurants and bars:	Different types of cuisine e.g. Italian, Chinese, German, Mexican and local Galician restaurants. Most restaurants in old quarter. Lots of bars around the city.

Sports and leisure facilities:	18-hole golf course. 6 museums including San Telmo museum. Aquarium. Casino. City concert hall – concerts, operas and plays. Also Jazz, Film and Music festivals. Several parks and gardens. Mount Igeldo attraction park with over 30 attractions.

Transport:	Public transport Train services from Bilbao, Barcelona and Madrid. Buses from Madrid, Barcelona, Bilbao, Pamplona, Valencia, Alicante and Salamanca.	Roads A-8 from Bilbao. A-63 from Irun. N-1 from Madrid.

Crime rate:	Low
Main types of employment:	Agriculture and fishing industry.
Future plans:	None.
Yield range:	5.4%–6.4%

Type of property:	Entry price	Rent – school holiday peak	Rent – peak	Rent – off peak	Average annual yield
2 bed apartment	214,862	600	480	288	6.4%
3 bed apartment	268,578	720	576	346	6.1%
3 bed townhouse	402,866	960	768	461	5.4%
Villa	472,696	1,260	1,008	605	6.1%

Demand for letting:	School holiday peak High		Peak High		Off peak High

Finance and leisure scores:	Financial (out of 5) 3	Leisure (out of 5) 2	Total (out of 10) 5

Flights scheduled from:	Gatwick, Heathrow, London City, Stansted, Bristol, Newquay, Plymouth, Southampton, Birmingham, Newcastle, Teesside, Manchester, Isle of Man, Aberdeen, Edinburgh, Glasgow, Inverness, Guernsey, Jersey, Leeds/Bradford, Belfast City, Belfast International, Dublin.

Typical cost of flights:	School holiday peak £136–270		Peak £101–200		Off peak £76–150

Operators:	Iberia, BA, BMI, Al Italia.

| Description: | San Sebastian, locally known as Donostia, lies 21 km west of the French border. The city is set in a circular bay (La Concha), on the edge of thick forests. There are three beaches: Concha, the most famous one; Ondarreta and Zurriola (also called Gros). Concha and Ondarreta from a bay adorned with Santa Clara Island.
Sights to see include Miramar Palace, which is between the Concha and Ondarreta beaches, the 19th century Buen Pastor cathedral, Castillo de la Santa Cruz de la Mota, and Aiete's Palace in the Aiete neighbourhood. The city also has an old quarter (Parte Vieja).
San Sebastian is not the obvious choice for buying a holiday home but it has the climate for a holiday home for nearly half the year. The area is driveable to (around 11 hours) so can be easily accessed without the need to book flights for the whole family. It has some of the facilities you would find at the better southern resorts but not all. It has some facilites that you wouldn't find in these southern resorts such as classical Spanish cinemas and traditional religious festivals.
Prices aren't necessarily cheap with entry prices starting from 200,000 Euros. The level of English spoken is lower than the resorts down south. Demand for rental properties is consistent throughout the year from the French as well as the English. |
|---|---|

Hot website:	http://www.terra.es/personal6/aintzane1/san-sebastian.html

Estate Agents:	**Name**	**Address**	**Tel**	**Web**
	Spanish Property Network	The Knowe, Barrhill, Dalbeattie DG5 4JD	01556 610712 Fax: 01556 610712	Not disclosed

Estate Agents:	Name	Address	Tel	Web
	Taylor Woodrow European Dept	2 Princes Way, Solihull, West Midlands B91 3ES	0121 600 8000 Fax: 0121 600 8001	Not disclosed
	Atlas International	Atlas House, Station Road, Dorking, Surrey RH4 1EB	01306 879899 Fax: 01306 877441	Not disclosed
	Bellamy Marks International	22 Markhouse Avenue, London E17 8AZ	0845 090 0199	Not disclosed
Letting Agents:	Name	Address	Tel	Web
	Spanish Property Network	The Knowe, Barrhill, Dalbeattie DG5 4JD	01556 610712 Fax: 01556 610712	Not disclosed
	Taylor Woodrow European Dept	2 Princes Way, Solihull, West Midlands B91 3ES	0121 600 8000 Fax: 0121 600 8001	Not disclosed
	Atlas International	Atlas House, Station Road, Dorking, Surrey RH4 1EB	01306 879899 Fax: 01306 877441	Not disclosed
	Bellamy Marks International	22 Markhouse Avenue, London E17 8AZ	0845 090 0199	Not disclosed

Santander, Cantabria

Investor profile:	Worker, Business					
Category:	B					
Population:	Total 180,000			British 2,000		
Climate:	Hours of sunshine per day in summer	Days of rain per year	Average spring air temp.	Average summer air temp.	Average autumn air temp.	Average winter air temp.	Average water temp.
	7	160	15	22	18	12	14

Proximity to:	Airport 4 miles (Santander)	Beach 0.25 miles	Nearest city Santander
Educational facilities:	Number of universities 2	Number of international schools 1	Number of private schools 3
Health services:	Number of public hospitals 1	Number of private hospitals 2	Number of private clinics 7

Shopping:	Number of shopping centres 3	Number of markets 2

Restaurants and bars:	Many tapas bars in Cañadio and Santa Lucia. Traditional and local cuisine found in Varda district.
Sports and leisure facilities:	Golf courses. Prehistoric and Archaeological museum. Prehistorical Caves of Altamira. Art museum (Museo de Bellas Artes). Maritime museum with aquarium (Museo Maritimo del Cantabrico). Caberceno National Park. Large casino near royal palace at El Sardinero. Zoo at Magdalena Park. Matalenas Park and Gardens at Cabo Menor cape. Lots of nightclubs in Plaza de Cañadio area. Also public golf course, athletic track and a small zoo in Matalenas Park. Classical music recitals and ballet performances at the Palacio de Festivales.

Transport:	Public transport	Roads
	RENFE train services from Madrid, Palencia, Reinosa, Segovia and Vallodolid. FEVE train services from Bilbao, Oviedo, Torrelavega and Unquera. Bus services from other coastal towns and resorts including Bilbao and San Sebastian. Frequent buses within Santander itself. Boat services every 15 minutes across the bay.	N-634 from Oviedo and C-642 and N-634 from A Coruña. N-623 from Burgos.

Crime rate:	Low				
Main types of employment:	Agriculture.				
Future plans:	Completion of A-8 motorway to Asturias.				
Yield range:	11.9%–13.4%				
Type of property:	Entry price	Rent – school holiday peak	Rent – peak	Rent – off peak	Average annual yield
2 bed apartment	82,874	455	364	218	12.5%
3 bed apartment	99,448	546	437	262	12.5%
3 bed townhouse	124,311	728	582	349	13.4%
Villa	182,323	956	764	459	11.9%
Demand for letting:	School holiday peak High		Peak High		Off peak High
Finance and leisure scores:	Financial (out of 5) 5		Leisure (out of 5) 1		Total (out of 10) 6
Flights scheduled from:	Gatwick, Heathrow, Bristol, Newquay, Plymouth, Birmingham, Newcastle, Manchester, Aberdeen, Edinburgh, Glasgow, Inverness, Guernsey, Jersey, Leeds/Bradford.				
Typical cost of flights:	School holiday peak £294–725		Peak £218–537		Off peak £164–403
Operators:	Iberia, BA, Air Europa.				
Description:	Santander is the capital city of Cantabria, located within a bay and with a large port (recently expanded) and old quarter. The nearby resort of El Sardinero is 2 miles away with 4 sandy beaches: Camello, Concha, Primera and Segunda. Sights to visit include the cathedral with Gothic crypt. The medieval town of Santillana del Mar is also a few kilometres away. Events include the International Music Festival in August.				

Property is more expensive in Santander than the Asturias and Galicia. Visitors numbers are consistent and therefore demand is consistent for rental properties. There isn't much property development going on so your purchase is likely to be a re-sale property. The yields are slightly better than average so you can be assured that this area would be one of the safer investments.

There aren't many British here. It's unlikely there will be either unless everyone follows this bit of advice in the book! This is part of the appeal of this area to some investors. It has great connections to the rest of Spain and the public transport is quite developed compared to other areas. Owning a car is not necessary here.

There are plenty of employment opportunities in the agricultural sector. It's a great place to live and work. There are many facilities as can be seen in the section above. The crime rate is also extremely low compared to anywhere in Europe. This makes this part of Spain unique considering Spain's wider problem of petty crime.

Hot website:	http://santander-spain.travel-holiday-guide.co.uk/			
Estate Agents:	**Name**	**Address**	**Tel**	**Web**
	García-Repetto	Lealtad, 19 – E, Cantabria Santander	0034 942 314 367/Fax: 0034 942 224 409	http://www.angelfire.com/ga/ApiRepetto/index.html email: apirepetto@netscape.net
	Cantabria Rustica	Jose Mª Pereda 37 Torrelavega	0034 609 008 070/Fax: 0034 942 086 046	http://www cantabria rustica.com email: manuel@cantabria rustica.com
	Morris Properties Overseas	Anchor House, Anchor Road, Aldridge, West Midlands WS9 8PW	01922 744459 Fax: 01922 744461	Not disclosed
	Yes Property International	Legend House, 10 Market Place, Faversham, Kent ME13 7AG	0870 300 4260	Not disclosed
Letting Agents:	**Name**	**Address**	**Tel**	**Web**
	García-Repetto	Lealtad, 19 – E Cantabria Santander	0034 942 314 367/Fax: 0034 942 224 409	http://www.angelfire.com/ga/ApiRepetto/index.html email: apirepetto@netscape.net

Torremolinos, Costa del Sol

Investor profile:	Retirement, Worker, Holiday, Business		
Category:	B		
Population:	**Total** 42,000		**British** 4,000

Climate:	Hours of sunshine per day in summer	Days of rain per year	Average spring air temp.	Average summer air temp.	Average autumn air temp.	Average winter air temp.	Average water temp.
	11	45	21	28	24	16	20

Proximity to:	Airport 6 miles (Malaga)	Beach 0.25 miles	Nearest city Malaga (9 miles)
Educational facilities:	Number of universities 0	Number of international schools 1	Number of private schools 2
Health services:	Number of public hospitals 0	Number of private hospitals 0	Number of private clinics 4

Shopping:	Number of shopping centres 0	Number of markets 1

Restaurants and bars:	Over 500 restaurants and bars serving a great variety of cuisine. Seafood restaurants specialising in fried fish along the seafront (La Carihuela). Tapas bars in old quarter.
Sports and leisure facilities:	Large public sports centre with athletics track. Parador del Golf golf club. Aguapark water-park (open in Summer only). Ritmo a Caballo Equestrian Ballet. Gay bars and nightclubs. Puerto Marina nearby with bars, restaurants and nightclubs.

Transport:	**Public transport** Train from Malaga or Fuengirola to Paseo de la Nogalera. Frequent bus services from nearby towns to Calle Hoya.	**Roads** N-340 from Malaga, exiting at Palacio de Congreso.

Crime rate:	Low.
Main types of employment:	Tourist and service sectors.
Future plans:	New construction around Los Alamos area, between town centre and airport. Otherwise very restricted.
Yield range:	8.3%–9.8%

Type of property:	Entry price	Rent – school holiday peak	Rent – peak	Rent – off peak	Average annual yield
2 bed apartment	96,000	412	330	198	9.8%
3 bed apartment	120,000	494	396	237	9.4%
3 bed townhouse	180,000	659	527	316	8.3%
Villa	211,200	865	692	415	9.3%

Demand for letting:	School holiday peak High	Peak Medium	Off peak Low

Finance and leisure scores:	Financial (out of 5) 5	Leisure (out of 5) 3	Total (out of 10) 8

Flights scheduled from:	Gatwick, Heathrow, London City, Luton, Stansted, Bristol, Cardiff, Exeter, Newquay, Plymouth, Bournemouth, Southampton, Birmingham, East Midlands, Humberside, Newcastle, Teesside, Blackpool, Isle of Man, Liverpool, Manchester, Aberdeen, Edinburgh, Glasgow, Inverness, Belfast City, Belfast International, Derry, Cork, Dublin, Guernsey, Jersey, Norwich, Leeds/Bradford.

Typical cost of flights:	School holiday peak £201–320	Peak £149–237	Off peak £112–178

Operators:	Monarch, Swiss International, BA, Air France, Excel Airways, Futura, Thomas Cook, Astraeus, Air 2000, My Travel, Easyjet.

| Description: | Torremolinos is the busiest resort in the Costa del Sol and the third busiest in Spain. It is also one of the oldest resorts, having been developed in the early 1960s. The majority of the area is characterised by high-rise hotel and apartment blocks, although there are also some newer residential areas with townhouses and villas to the west. The beaches are clean and well-maintained and there is an abundance of bars, restaurants and nightlife so it makes a great location for a holiday home.
Property prices are relatively cheap, with the exception of the Montemar area. The cheaper properties are available in the 1960's and 1970's-built apartment blocks on a re-sale basis. Surprisingly the rental prices are lower than its neighbours but this is probably due to the over supply of rental properties. If you want to command a decent rent for the majority of the peak periods then go for the newer developments. If you want to take a risk and not too bothered about the financial considerations then bargain properties can be had simply to be your holiday home.
Because of the well developed property market in this area try and get the local press. There are many properties advertised here. Consider advertising in the local press expressing your wants and what you are willing to spend. The property market is fluid here. There are always buyers as well as sellers looking to make that deal. |
|---|---|

Hot website:	http://www.infotu.com/toingle.htm

Estate Agents:	Name	Address	Tel	Web
	Coast & Country – Property Sales & Rentals	Avda. de España 12, 29620 Torremolinos, Málaga	0034 952 384 192/Fax: 0034 952 377 230	http://www. coastcountry property.com/ email: info@ coastcountry property.com
	Pedevillas Inmobiliarias	Plaza Costa del Sol, 3 Torremolinos	0034 952 383 466/Fax: 0034 952 380 610	http://www. pedevilla.com/ cliente/ escaparate/ paginas/default. asp email: pedevilla. tor@pedevilla. com
	Torremolinos Estate	C/ Carmen Montes, L-2 Torremolinos	Not disclosed	email: info@ inmocostadel sol.com
	Haart	P.O. Box 5995 Colchester Essex CO3 3WR	0845 600 7778	http://www.tmx haart.co.uk/ email: webmaster@ haart.co.uk
Letting Agents:	Name	Address	Tel	Web
	Coast & Country – Property Sales & Rentals	Avda. de España 12, 29620 Torremolinos, Málaga	0034 952 384 192/Fax: 0034 952 377 230	http://www. coastcountry property.com/ email: info@ coastcountry property.com

Torrevieja, Costa Blanca			
Investor profile:	Retirement, Worker, Holiday, Business		
Category:	C		
Population:	Total 72,000		British 20,000

Climate:	Hours of sunshine per day in summer	Days of rain per year	Average spring air temp.	Average summer air temp.	Average autumn air temp.	Average winter air temp.	Average water temp.
	11	42	21	30	24	17	18

Proximity to:	Airport 22 miles (Alicante)	Beach 0.25 miles	Nearest city 29 miles (Alicante)
Educational facilities:	Number of universities 0	Number of international schools 1	Number of private schools 2
Health services:	Number of public hospitals 0	Number of private hospitals 1	Number of private clinics 4

Shopping:	Number of shopping centres 0	Number of markets 2

Restaurants and bars:	Wide variety of cuisine available. Local speciality is seafood. Live entertainment bars.
Sports and leisure facilities:	Sports centre with athletics track. Private sports centres. Tennis clubs. Flying club. 1,500-berth marina with renowned yacht club. Diving and windsurfing clubs. 4 golf courses in area. Water-park north of Torrevieja open in Summer. Theatre. Casino. 3 museums including sea and salt museum.

Transport:	Public transport Bus services within most of the town, and to surrounding areas including Alicante.	Roads N-332 from Valencia, Benidorm and Alicante.

Crime rate:	High
Main types of employment:	Mostly tourist and service sectors. However many foreign companies situated in the area.
Future plans:	New hotels/apartments/houses being constructed. Town is rapidly expanding.
Yield range:	5.9%–6.9%

Type of property:	Entry price	Rent – school holiday peak	Rent – peak	Rent – off peak	Average annual yield
2 bed apartment	105,720	318	254	153	6.9%
3 bed apartment	132,150	382	305	183	6.6%
3 bed townhouse	198,225	509	407	244	5.9%
Villa	232,584	668	534	321	6.5%

Demand for letting:	School holiday peak High	Peak High	Off peak Medium

Finance and leisure scores:	Financial (out of 5) 2	Leisure (out of 5) 5	Total (out of 10) 7

Flights scheduled from:	Gatwick, Heathrow, London City, Luton, Stansted, Bristol, Cardiff, Exeter, Newquay, Plymouth, Bournemouth, Southampton, Birmingham, East Midlands, Humberside, Newcastle, Teesside, Blackpool, Isle of Man, Liverpool, Manchester, Aberdeen, Edinburgh, Glasgow, Inverness, Belfast City, Belfast International, Derry, Cork, Dublin, Guernsey, Jersey, Norwich, Leeds/Bradford.

Typical cost of flights:	School holiday peak £192–485	Peak £142–359	Off peak £107–269

Operators:	Monarch, Iberia, BA, BMI, Air-Berlin, Thomas Cook, Easyjet, Flybe, Excel Airways, Britannia Airways, Futura, European Air Charter, My Travel, Astraeus, Air2000.

Description:	A popular tourist destination in the Costa Blanca, Torrevieja is a busy resort still being developed. It is situated within 2 large natural salt lakes called 'Salterns of Torrevieja'. Sights to see include the large Moorish tower (Torre del Moro) and Church of the Immaculate Conception. There are also many beaches and amenities.
	It can be lively, noisy and crowded, particularly in Summer. Also there is a rising crime rate involving burglary and theft. However the area has the cheapest property on the Costa Blanca and as the town is constantly developing, property prices are expected to rise. Yields are not that brilliant but the prospect for capital growth compensates for this. If you're looking for a holiday home that will pay for itself for 5 years and then to sell on to make a profit then this area will meet your goal.
	Funnily enough Torrevieja is also particularly popular with visitors with allergic and respiratory problems, who are thought to benefit from the salty environment but don't rely on this market to make your investment decision!

Hot website:	http://www.costa-blanca-torrevieja.to/

Estate Agents:	Name	Address	Tel	Web
	Panorama Golf	Urb. Panaroma Glf, Apartado de Correos 312, 03180 Torrevieja, Alicante	0034 609 536 331/Fax: 0034 609 500 966	Not disclosed
	Astur Mar	C/Guardamar 8 Torrevieja	0034 965 707 916/Fax: 0034 965 707 916	http://www. casaspania.com email: astur_mar @terra.es
	Sun & Sea International	Torrevieja	0034 617 952 613	http://www. sun-sea-international. com email: info@ sun-sea-international. com
	Sol Partners	Avda. de Francia, 60 – 1ºD La Mata Torrevieja	0034 966 925 022/Fax: 0034 966 921 320	email: mle 24549@terra.es
Letting Agents:	Name	Address	Tel	Web
	AMATorrevieja 2010	C/ Pedro Lorca, 71 – Bajo Torrevieja	0034 965 706 817/Fax: 0034 965 706 817	email: amatorrevieja 2010@hotmail. com
	Costa Blanca Rentals	Suite 173, Ctra. La Nao 71 03730 Javca	0034 966 460 681/Fax: 0034 966 460 681	http://www. cberentals.com email: info@ cberentals.com
	EuroCasa Gestion Inmobiliaria	Aptdo Correos 2053 Alicante	0034 655 169 971	email: daniel combret@ yahoo.es
	Sajonia	Avda. Alfonso el Sabio, 16, 8-Izq Alicante	0034 965 230 627/Fax: 0034 965 230 627	email: sajonia21 @yahoo.es

Tossa de Mar, Costa Brava

Investor profile:	Retirement, Worker, Holiday, Business		
Category:	B		
Population:	Total 15,000		British 1,000

Climate:	Hours of sunshine per day in summer	Days of rain per year	Average spring air temp.	Average summer air temp.	Average autumn air temp.	Average winter air temp.	Average water temp.
	9	96	16	26	20	13	17

Proximity to:	Airport 22 miles (Girona)	Beach 0.25 miles	Nearest city 24 miles (Girona)
Educational facilities:	Number of universities 0	Number of international schools 0	Number of private schools 2
Health services:	Number of public hospitals 0	Number of private hospitals 0	Number of private clinics 2

Shopping:	Number of shopping centres 0	Number of markets 2

Restaurants and bars:	Over 100 restaurants offering local, Indian, Chinese, Italian and Mexican cuisine. Fast food also available.	
Sports and leisure facilities:	Anna Esteve Llach sports pavilion and football ground. Skating rink. Mountain biking club. Canoeing, sailing, windsurfing and water-skiing at Cala Llevado sports centre. Parasailing at Platja Gran and Porto Pi beaches. Scuba-diving centres. 8 tennis clubs. Boat excursions along coast. Museum. Sa Riera Park and Gardens. Youth Club. 29 bars and 4 nightclubs including open-air Catxa Club.	

Transport:	**Public transport** Bus services from Barcelona, Girona, Lloret de Mar and Blanes. Train services from Barcelona (including airport).	**Roads** N-II motorway from Girona and Barcelona.
Crime rate:	Low	
Main types of employment:	Tourism and service sector.	
Future plans:	None	
Yield range:	11.4%–13.4%	

Type of property:	Entry price	Rent – school holiday peak	Rent – peak	Rent – off peak	Average annual yield
2 bed apartment	128,678	759	607	364	13.4%
3 bed apartment	160,848	911	729	437	12.9%
3 bed townhouse	243,710	1,214	972	583	11.4%
Villa	283,093	1,594	1,275	765	12.8%

Demand for letting:	School Holiday Peak High		Peak High		Off peak Low

Finance and leisure scores:	Financial (out of 5) 4	Leisure (out of 5) 4	Total (out of 10) 8

Flights scheduled from:	Gatwick, Heathrow, Luton, Stansted, Bristol, Cardiff, Newquay, Plymouth, Birmingham, East Midlands, Newcastle, Teesside, Isle of Man, Manchester, Aberdeen, Edinburgh, Glasgow, Inverness, Belfast City, Belfast International, Guernsey, Jersey, Leeds/Bradford.

Typical cost of flights:	School holiday peak £100–383	Peak £74–284	Off peak £56–213

Operators:	BA, Iberia, Air2000, Thomas Cook, Britannia Airways, My Travel.

Description:	Tossa de Mar is a built-up and developed resort, popular with British package tourists like Lloret de Mar. Unlike Lloret de Mar however, this resort has more of a Spanish atmosphere. The area consists of 2 main beaches (Mar Grand and La Bauma) surrounding a medieval town. The town also has an old quarter surrounded by 12th century walls.
	Yields are good but the scope for capital growth is limited. There are no future building plans that I could find – but don't let this put you off. There's lots to do, the climate's good and it's clean. It's also cheap to get here.
	With all holiday homes you have to balance the facilities offered by the area with the amount of return you expect from the property. This area can offer you a great holiday home and will pay for itself but don't expect more than that. If you're in it for the long term then there could be good returns to be had within the 10–20 year timescale. It is an attractive resort and this, some day, will be recognised.

Hot website:	http://www.infotossa.com/

Estate Agents:	Name	Address	Tel	Web
	Tossa de Mar	C/ Capità Mestres s/n Tossa de Mar Gerona	0034 972 342 815/Fax: 0034 972 342 641	http://www. tossa-de-mar. com email: Info@ Tossa-de-Mar. com

Estate Agents:	Name	Address	Tel	Web
	The Prestige Property Group	No address	01935 817188 Fax: 01935 817199	http://www. prestige property.co.uk email: sales@ prestige property.co.uk
	Inmobiliaria Peñarroya S.A.	Urbanizacion Reserva de Marbella, s/n 29600 Marbella (Malaga)	0034 952 835 286	Not disclosed
	Directo Constructor	Carretera de Blanes 101 Lloret de Mar 17310-Girona	0034 972 360 615/Fax: 0034 972 373 013	http://www. directo constructor.com/ en/empresa.asp email: info@ directo constructor.com
Letting Agents:	Name	Address	Tel	Web
	Universal Holiday Centre	C/ Bruselas, 39 Salou (Tarragona)	0034 977 353 010/Fax: 0034 977 353 448	http://www. universalholiday centre.com/ indexb.html email: info@ universalholiday centre.com
	Tossa de Mar	C/ Capità Mestres s/n Tossa de Mar Gerona	0034 972 342 815/Fax: 0034 972 342 641	http://www. tossa-de-mar. com email: Info@ Tossa-de- Mar.com

Valencia		
Investor profile:	Worker, Business	
Category:	A	
Population:	Total 740,000	British 4,000

Climate:	Hours of sunshine per day in summer	Days of rain per year	Average spring air temp.	Average summer air temp.	Average autumn air temp.	Average winter air temp.	Average water temp.
	11	42	21	30	24	17	18

Proximity to:	Airport 5 miles (Valencia)	Beach 0.5 miles	Nearest city Valencia
Educational facilities:	Number of universities 2	Number of international schools 5	Number of private schools 6
Health services:	Number of public hospitals 2	Number of private hospitals 2	Number of private clinics 12

Shopping:	Number of shopping centres 5	Number of markets 3
Restaurants and bars:	Although a wide choice of different cuisine is available, Valencia offers a good selection of restaurants specialising in local cuisine, particularly paella.	
Sports and leisure facilities:	Public and private sport centres. Athletics stadium. Marinas nearby and marina in port. Royal Sailing Club. 4 golf courses in and around city, including El Saler Golf Course. GR-7 and GR-8 hiking paths. Canoeing. Paragliding. City of Arts and Sciences with big auditorium and waterside architecture. Theatres, opera, ballet. Museum. IMAX cinema. 2 cinemas showing English-language films. L'Oceanografic underwater centre. Nightclubs situated on outskirts of city, on the Valencia-Cullera road and in Calle Juan Llorens.	

Transport:	Public transport Trains from Madrid, Alicante and Murcia. Coaches from surrounding towns. Metro train service with 3 lines within the city. Several bus routes across city.	Roads N-III motorway from Madrid. A-7 motorway from Barcelona and Costa Blanca. A-92, N-340 and A-7 from Granada.
Crime rate:	High	
Main types of employment:	Mostly professional.	

Future plans:	Continued restoration of port.				
Yield range:	8.1%–9.5%				
Type of property:	Entry price	Rent – school holiday peak	Rent – peak	Rent – off peak	Average annual yield
2 bed apartment	96,000	399	319	192	9.5%
3 bed apartment	120,000	479	383	230	9.1%
3 bed townhouse	180,000	638	511	306	8.1%
Villa	211,200	838	670	402	9.0%
Demand for letting:	School holiday peak High		Peak High		Off peak High
Finance and leisure scores:	Financial (out of 5) 4		Leisure (out of 5) 5		Total (out of 10) 9
Flights scheduled from:	Gatwick, Heathrow, London City, Stansted, Bristol, Cardiff, Newquay, Plymouth, Southampton, Birmingham, Humberside, Newcastle, Teesside, Isle of Man, Manchester, Aberdeen, Edinburgh, Glasgow, Inverness, Belfast City, Belfast International, Guernsey, Jersey, Norwich, Leeds/Bradford.				
Typical cost of flights:	School holiday peak £174–296		Peak £129–219		Off peak £97–164
Operators:	BA, Swiss International, Air France.				
Description:	Valencia is Spain's third largest city and is situated on the east coast. It has a thriving business district which makes Valencia one of the most important cities in the whole of the Mediterranean. It's total catchment population is in excess of 1.5 million if you take in to account the surrounding towns that feed off the commercial success of the city. It is a well connected city through road, rail, port and airport links and therefore has a far more cosmopolitan feel than its neighbouring cities. Valencia also enjoys an even climate through the year averaging out at around 17°C so summers are not too hot neither winters too cold. When you arrive there it's obvious that it places the conduct of business high in its priorities. It used to be the financial capital of Europe 500 years ago and you can see that it is trying to regain that title now. There are futuristic exhibition halls that attract other businesses around the world to congregate and trade. The futurism doesn't stop there however. Even the arts and leisure buildings are all being redesigned to meet the demands of the 21st century. It has its own dialect (Valenciano) which is a form of Catalan and is highly used – but the use of English is higher in Valencia than other cities. It is a lively city and a noisy one! Crime rates are high but it's not serious crime, just petty theft so be sure to go for a site with CCTV or 24-hour security guards.				

	There is lots of property for sale (mostly apartments), and cheap houses can be found on the city outskirts. It also has 2 universities so there is a demand for student rentals for most of the year.			
Hot website:	http://www.cuspideuk.com/info_Valencia.htm			
Estate Agents:	Name	Address	Tel	Web
	Spanish Dreams	Camino Assagador 24, 45758 Barx, la Drova, Valencia	0034 962 807 426	Not disclosed
	Costa Spanish Eyes	Ausias March 33B, Oliva, 46780 Valencia	0034 962 839 863/Fax: 0034 962 839 863	Not disclosed
	Cuspide	C/ Jativa 4 esc, drcha 2 pt 3 Valencia	963104500	http://www.cuspide.es/english/ofertas.htm email: valencia@cuspide.es
	DLR Properties Overseas	5 Manor Parade, Brightlingsea, Colchester, Essex CO7 0UD	01206 303 049 Fax: 01206 306 090	Not disclosed
Letting Agents:	Name	Address	Tel	Web
	Spanish Dreams	Camino Assagador 24, 45758 Barx, la Drova, Valencia	0034 962 807 426	Not disclosed
	Costa Spanish Eyes	Ausias March 33B, Oliva, 46780 Valencia	0034 962 839 863/Fax: 0034 962 839 863	Not disclosed

Other Services

The author also offers a portfolio building service to clients of all sizes. He will help with:

■ Sourcing the right properties tailored to your own strategy.

■ Raising the cheapest finance to purchase the properties.

■ Finding the right tenants.

■ The ongoing maintenance of the properties.

If you are thinking of building a portfolio or need help expanding your portfolio then contact:

Ajay Ahuja BSc ACA
Accountants Direct
99 Moreton Road
Ongar
Essex
CM5 0AR

Tel: 0800 652 3979
Fax: 01277 362563
Email: emergencyaccountants@yahoo.co.uk
Web: www.buytolethotspots.com

Index of Property Hotspots

If you want to know how...

■ To buy a home in the sun, and let it out

■ To move overseas, and work well with the people who live there

■ To get the job you want, in the career you like

■ To plan a wedding, and make the Best Man's speech

■ To build your own home, or manage a conversion

■ To buy and sell houses, and make money from doing so

■ To gain new skills and learning, at a later time in life

■ To empower yourself, and improve your lifestyle

■ To start your own business, and run it profitably

■ To prepare for your retirement, and generate a pension

■ To improve your English, or write a PhD

■ To be a more effective manager, and a good communicator

■ To write a book and get it published

If you want to know how to do all these things and much, much more...

howtobooks

Practical books that inspire

If you want to know how ... to make money from property

"Many of the world's richest people have made their fortunes from property. Now you can make money from property too – if you are careful. This book will show you how to spot property investment opportunities and how to avoid all the common mistakes. Whether your objective is to add a little to your income in retirement or become a full-time property developer, this book will show you how."

Adam Walker

How to Make Money from Property
The expert guide to property investment
Adam Walker

"Invest in this book today and make it your first valuable property investment." – *Amazon review*

"A guide to many different ways of making money from property, from letting a room to buying land for development" – landlordzone.co.uk

"I was already considering investing in the property ... initially sceptical, I found this book to be my first step on the property investment ladder." – *Amazon review*

ISBN 1 85703 627 1

If you want to know how ... to retire to Spain

"Possibly for the first time in years we are really happy. Stress is a distant memory. We do have less disposable income than we had in London, but we don't need it. With just a bit more than the minimum amount of money to cover utility bills, clothes and food we can and do live very well. We reflect often on how wise our decision was to move to Spain."

Tom Provan

Gone to Spain
How you, too, can realise your dream of living in Spain
Tom Provan

Tom Provan, after a long and successful career in marketing and PR took the decision to leave England and move – lock, stock, barrel and dog – to Spain. In this book you'll learn from his experiences. Some are very positive, some are frustrating and some are very funny. But if you are contemplating making the same move there is valuable information here that will help you decide whether this is the right decision for you.

ISBN 1 85703 928 9

If you want to know how ... to live and work in Spain

"There is only one way to be sure of what Spain has to offer: come and see it for yourself. Going to Spain to work, for a long-term stay, or for retirement can be a step into the unknown. But if some simple preparation is undertaken it can be a step into sunshine and happiness."

Harry King

Going to Live in Spain
A practical guide to enjoying a new lifestyle in the sun
Harry King

"Spain has long been a popular destination. This book covers all aspects of relocating there, throwing up information on living in Spain, from its cultural history to the ins and outs of its current economy, the documentation you'll need, and, of course, the all-important climate." – *The Mirror*

"Tips on how to get the most out of this vibrant country so that you can enjoy your new life to the full." – *Sunday Telegraph*

ISBN 1 85703 875 4

If you want to know how ... to retire abroad

"Just because you're retired doesn't mean that you are content to sit back and reminisce about the past. Instead you are determined to live life to the full and fulfil as many of your aspirations as you can. These may well involve spending time in a different – probably warmer – clime for part or even all of the year. This book offers suggestions and advice and also provides a wide range of contacts – from estate agents to embassies, from furniture removers to financial advisers. I hope that this guide will prove indispensable in your decision making, steering you successfully in the right direction."

Roger Jones

Retire Abroad
Your complete guide to a new life in the sun
Roger Jones

"Provides advice and hard facts on finding a location, getting there, and coping once you're there – and even contains advice if you decide you want to come back! Invaluable chapters include 'What You Need to Know Before Proceeding' and 'How Much Will It Cost?' The appendices are packed with useful addresses and phone numbers." – *The Mirror*

"... the book contains much thought-provoking information for those considering spending their golden years abroad." – *French Property News*

"This guide is an excellent staring point. It represents a very modest investment when one considers the expensive and/or ghastly mistakes that may ensue if important points are overlooked." – *Living France*

ISBN 1 85703 782 0

We've published a lot of books addressing all sorts of problems and opportunities that people come across.

How To Books are available through all good bookshops, or you can order direct from us through Grantham Book Services.

Tel: +44 (0)1476 541080
Fax: +44 (0)1476 541061
Email: orders@gbs.tbs-ltd.co.uk

Or via our website

www.howtobooks.co.uk

To order via any of these methods please quote the title(s) of the book(s) and your credit card number together with an expiry date.

For further information about our books and catalogue, please contact:

How To Books
3 Newtec Place
Magdalen Road
Oxford OX4 1RE

Visit our website at

www.howtobooks.co.uk

Or you can contact us by email at info@howtobooks.co.uk